BIOLOGY IN PRACTICE

FOR STANDARD GRADE

by

Johanna Carrie
James Dorward
John Robertson
Livingston Russell

Oxford University Press 1990

Oxford University Press, Walton Street, Oxford OX2 6DP

Oxford   New York   Toronto
Delhi   Bombay   Calcutta   Madras   Karachi
Petaling Jaya   Singapore   Hong Kong   Tokyo
Nairobi   Dar es Salaam   Cape Town
Melbourne   Auckland

and associated companies in
Berlin   Ibadan

© Johanna Carrie, James Dorward, John Robertson,
Livingston Russell 1990

Oxford is a trade mark of Oxford University Press

ISBN 019 914 288 2

Typeset by Tradespools Ltd, Frome, Somerset
Printed in Singapore

Introduction

Biology in Practice can be used to introduce new concepts, to reinforce ideas which have been taught in class, to show applications of biological concepts, or to develop important information-handling skills.

The book is divided into chapters which correspond to the seven Standard Grade topics, and each chapter is made up of short articles dealing with different subjects. Interesting contexts introduce important ideas, and the questions which follow explore these ideas further.

The contents lists the skills which are practised in each article and indicates whether they are more suitable preparation for General or Credit level.

Acknowledgements

The publishers wish to thank the following for permission to reproduce photographs:

AFRC Engineering: p 98. **Barnaby's Picture Library**: p 99 (bottom). **Biophoto Associates**: pp 4, 18. **Sarah Brocklesby**: p 83. **John Cleare**: p 63. **Bruce Coleman**: p 88. **James Dorward**: pp 10, 11, 73, 76. **Sally & Richard Greenhill**: pp 46, 47. **Greenpeace**: pp 20, 23. **Frank Lane Picture Agency/William Broadhurst**: p 26. **D. Lees**: p 4. **Roger Tidman**: p 28. **Holt Studios**: pp 32, 88. **P. J. Palmer**: p 18. **Robert Arnold**: pp 4, 18. **John Lythgoe**: p 52. **Science Photo Library**: pp 41, 47, 85, 87, 88, 90, 91. **South American Pictures**: p 88. **Thames Water**: p 99.

The illustrations are by:

Bill Donohoe, Chris Duggan, Clive Goodyer, Ch'en Ling, Mark Rogerson, Simon Roulstone, Ursula Sieger, Tony Townsend, Pamela Venus and Galina Zolfaghari.

The authors wish to thank their colleagues, pupils and friends for helping to trial parts of the book. They also acknowledge the invaluable assistance and time willingly given by specialists who advised on suitable sources and helped obtain original data.

1 BIOSPHERE

1.1 **How many are there?** (G/C: Ca) 2
  Estimating by sampling techniques
1.2 **What's the viz?** (G/C: I, Co) 4
  Environmental factors and plankton
1.3 **Sampling trampling** (G: I, D, Co) 6
  Plant distribution
1.4 **A rock pool** (G/C: I, Co) 8
  Pyramid of numbers
1.5 **Tides and living conditions** (G/C: D, Co) 10
  Distribution of seaweeds
1.6 **Stocking a tropical aquarium** (G/C: D, Ca, Co) 12
  Planning for a mixed community
1.7 **The web** (G:D) 14
  Constructing a food web
1.8 **Pioneers** (G/C: I, Co) 15
  Growth of a population
1.9 **Sharing out the energy** (G/C: I, D, Co) 16
  Energy flow in a community
1.10 **Competition for survival** (G:I, C) 18
  Different species compete
1.11 **How many seeds should I sow?** (G:D, Co) 19
  Competition in one species
1.12 **Effects of acidity** (G:I, C) 20
  Acid rain in the environment
1.13 **Cause for complaint** (G/C: I, Ca, Co) 22
  Some causes of river pollution

2 PLANTS

2.1 **Uses of plants** (G:I, D) 24
  Sorting out plant products
2.2 **Oil from rape seed** (G/C: I, D, Co) 26
  Steps in the process
2.3 **Wonderful seaweeds** (G:I, C) 27
  Useful products from seaweeds
2.4 **How does your garden grow?** (G/C: E, Co) 28
  Factors affecting seed germination
2.5 **Light and shade** (G/C: I, Co) 30
  Photosynthesis in different plants
2.6 **A tale of two apples** (G:Co) 32
  Propagation in fruit crops
2.7 **Mars Station One** (G/C: I, D, Co) 34
  Factors affecting productivity in plants

3 ANIMALS

3.1 **Building bodies** (G/C: I) 36
  The chemistry of food
3.2 **Chance would be a fine thing** (G/C: I, Co) 38
  Adaptations for fertilization
3.3 **Voyage of the Gutbug** (G:I) 40
  Journey through the digestive system
3.4 **Producing convincing evidence** (G/C: E, Ca) 42
  Evaluating experimental procedures
3.5 **Replacing the kidneys** (G/C: I) 44
  Comparing kidney with dialysis
3.6 **Water, water everywhere** (G/C: I, C) 46
  Water balance
3.7 **Moonbugs** (G/C: I, D) 48
  Distribution of a species

4 CELLS

4.1 **Diffusion** (G:I) 50
  Substances in and out of cells
4.2 **Understanding osmosis** (G:I, D) 51
  Predicting water movement
4.3 **The salt marsh environment** (C:I, P) 52
  Distribution of salt-tolerant plants
4.4 **Energy use by cells** (G:D) 54
  Many uses of energy
4.5 **Give and take** (G/C: I, E) 56
  Heat balance
4.6 **Warming up** (G/C: D, P, I) 58
  Temperature and activity
4.7 **Testing Zoomo** (G/C: E) 59
  Fairness of advertisement trials
4.8 **Enzymes at work** (G/C: D, I) 60
  Changing activity levels

5 THE BODY IN ACTION

5.1 **Input = output?** (G: D, Co) 62
Individual energy balance
5.2 **Pick a packed lunch** (G:Co) 63
Planning for energy requirements
5.3 **Weight watchers** (G/C: I, Co) 64
Some problems of dieting
5.4 **Breathing bad air** (G/C: D, Co I) 66
Air composition and breathing rate
5.5 **Actively healthy?** (G:E) 68
Exercise and heart attacks
5.6 **I hurt it playing** (G/C: I, D) 70
Injuries in different sports
5.7 **Get a grip** (G/C: I, Co) 72
Muscle and endurance training
5.8 **More power to your heart** (G:I, Co) 74
Training of the heart
5.9 **Cycle to a stop** (G/C: I, Co) 76
Performance of heart and breathing

6 INHERITANCE

6.1 **What controls the result?** (G/C: D, I, Co) 78
Genetics versus environment
6.2 **Family and friends** (G:D, C) 80
Measuring degrees of similarity
6.3 **Robert the footballer** (G/C: D, P) 82
Inheritance pattern of Duchenne muscular dystrophy
6.4 **Lucky Stephanie** (G/C: E) 84
Diagnosis and inheritance pattern of thalassaemia
6.5 **Will baby be all right?** (G:I) 86
Diagnosis and decisions
6.6 **Improving plants** (G/C: I, E) 88
Design of a plant breeding programme
6.7 **Mutations** (G/C: I, E) 90
X-ray dose and mutations

7 BIOTECHNOLOGY

7.1 **Uses of microbes** (G:I) 92
Introducing biotechnology
7.2 **Cell growth** (G/C: I, D, Co) 94
Measuring microbe numbers
7.3 **The sewage works filter bed** (G/C: I, D, Co) 96
Microbes and sewage processing
7.4 **Gas from bugs** (G/C: I, D) 98
Sewage sludge digester
7.5 **Microbes for profit** (G/C: I, Co) 99
Batch and continuous processing
7.6 **Sewage and pollution** (G/C: I, Co) 100
Biotic index and oxygen levels
7.7 **The insulin story** (G:I) 102
Reprogramming microbes
7.8 **Should it be allowed?** (G:Co) 103
Pros and cons of genetic engineering

Numerical Answers 104

Index 107

Key

Level of Question
G = General level
C = Credit level
G/C = both levels

Skill
Ca = Calculation
Co = Drawing conclusions
D = Drawing diagrams/graphs/tables
E = Experimental design
I = Interpretation of diagrams/graphs/tables
P = Prediction

1.1 How many are there?

When studying the animals and plants in an area we often need to know how many of each type there are. If the area is small and the numbers are not too many, it may well be possible simply to count them all. It might be easy enough, for example, to count how many trees there are in a small garden or the number of crabs in a rockpool.

With larger areas and greater numbers simple counting can sometimes be practically impossible. No one would think seriously of counting directly the number of grass plants on a football field or the number of barnacles on a rocky beach!

One way around the problem of numbers too great to count is to use **sampling**. Instead of trying to count all the organisms in an area, we count how many there are in a small sample patch. We can then use this number to work out an estimate of roughly how many there are in the complete area.

Although estimating from a sample is much quicker and easier than a complete count, it is less accurate. Any estimate worked out from a sample assumes that the rest of the area is very much like the sample, and that any other sample would have a similar number of organisms in it.

With only one sample we cannot be sure that it is typical of the whole area. One way around this problem is to look at several samples and then calculate the average. We then use the average to estimate the total number. This makes our estimate more accurate and still saves us from having to do a complete count.

Try these problems, to see if you understand sampling.

1 A driver passes 50 street lamps in 1 km.
a) How many will he pass in 10 km?
b) How many will he pass in 50 km?
c) What are you assuming is true about the spacing of the lamps?

2 Ten 'seed' potatoes weigh a total of 500 g.
a) What does one potato weigh on average?
b) How many potatoes can a gardener plant from a bag weighing 3 kg?

3 Six bees are removed from a swarm and weighed. They weigh: 0.10 g, 0.08 g, 0.12 g, 0.13 g, 0.08 g, 0.09 g.
a) What is the average weight of one bee?
b) How many bees would be in a swarm weighing 2 kg?

4 In a 1 m × 1 m sample patch of a lawn, a girl counts four thistle plants (see Figure 1).
a) How many patches this size are there on a 10 m × 10 m lawn?
b) How many thistles would you expect to find on the whole lawn?
c) What are you assuming about all the other 1 m × 1 m patches?
d) What is the problem of using only one sample patch?

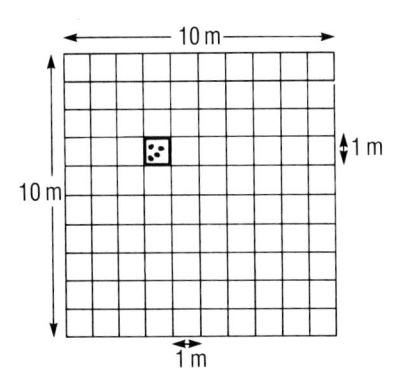

Figure 1. Lawn with thistles.

5 In a small wood 100 m wide and 200 m long, a forester chooses five sample areas, each area 10 m × 10 m square. The number of trees he finds in each area is shown in Figure 2.
a) What is the area of the wood in square metres?
b) What is the number of 10 m × 10 m areas in the whole wood?
c) What is the average number of trees per sample?
d) Estimate the number of trees in the whole wood.
e) What are you assuming is true about the distribution of the trees?
f) From the figures shown, do you think this assumption is reasonable? Explain your answer.

Figure 2. A small wood.

6 A rectangular pond is 10 m long, 5 m wide and 1 m deep (see Figure 3).
a) How many cubic metres of water are in the pond?
b) One cubic metre contains 1000 litres. How many litres are there in the pond?
c) A girl drops a 10 litre bucket into the pond four times to collect tadpoles. She catches 76 the first time, then 86, 64 and 74. What is the average number caught in 10 litres?
d) How many is this per litre?
e) How many tadpoles are probably in the pond?
f) Why can you not be certain how many there are?

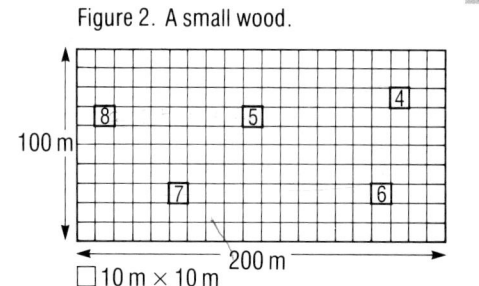

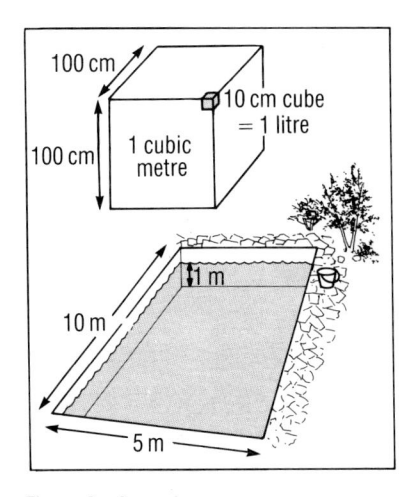

Figure 3. A pond.

BIOSPHERE

1.2 What's the viz?

The first question Scuba divers ask when they arrive at a dive site is 'What's the viz?' that is, the visibility underwater. How clear is the water? How far will they be able to see? The most glorious wreck or coral-encrusted cliff face will be practically invisible if the 'viz' is poor and the diver can see only one or two metres.

One of the causes of 'poor viz' is plankton – the millions of tiny floating animals and plants which inhabit the surface water of our seas. The water can often be turned to what looks like green-pea soup by a sudden growth of phytoplankton, plant plankton, near the surface.

These thousands of tiny one-celled plants not only make the water cloudy and hard to see through, but also filter out and absorb sunlight as it enters the water. Very little light reaches the deeper waters, so that even if the 'viz' is better down there, it is almost dark, even at midday!

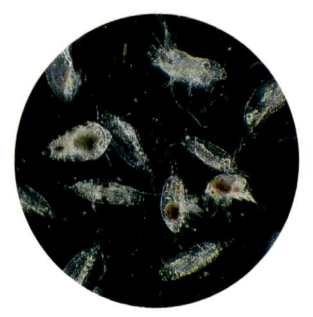

Plant plankton   Animal plankton

Figure 1 shows the changes in numbers of phytoplankton in the upper layers of the North Sea over a period of one year.

Figure 1.

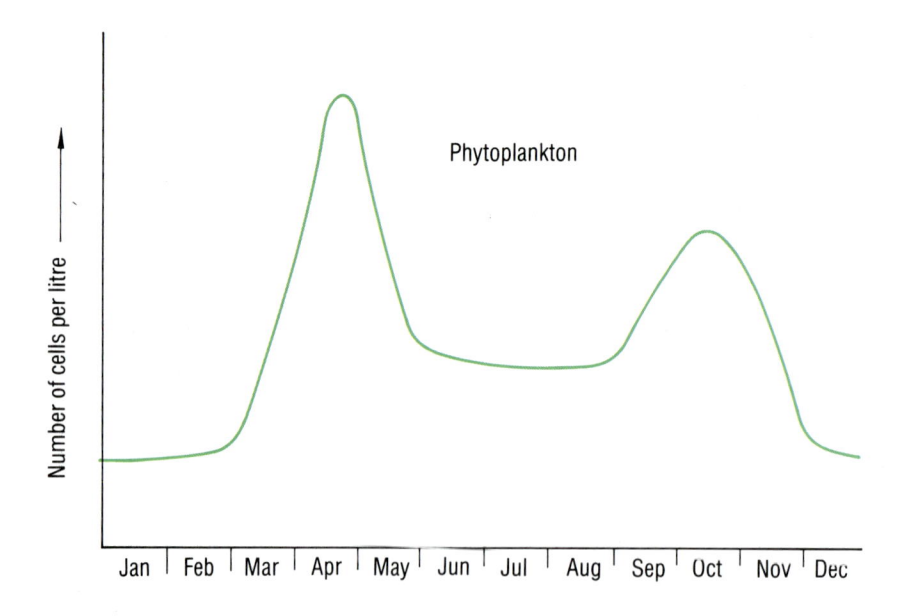

What causes these changes? To understand this we need to know what makes phytoplankton cells grow. Like all plants, they need light, carbon dioxide gas and minerals. Light comes from the sun, and carbon dioxide and minerals are dissolved in the sea water, especially in the deeper layers.

The supply of minerals is complicated by the behaviour of the sea itself. During the calm summer months (May to August), the upper layers of the sea warm up and tend to stay floating at the surface. They do not mix with the water from deeper down. The plankton live only in this warm upper layer. In summer, divers can often feel the sudden drop in temperature as they swim from the warm surface layer to the colder water deeper down.

In autumn and winter months, storms mix the warm surface waters with the colder mineral-rich waters from lower down.

Figure 2 shows the changes in light and mineral levels in the surface waters over the period of a year.

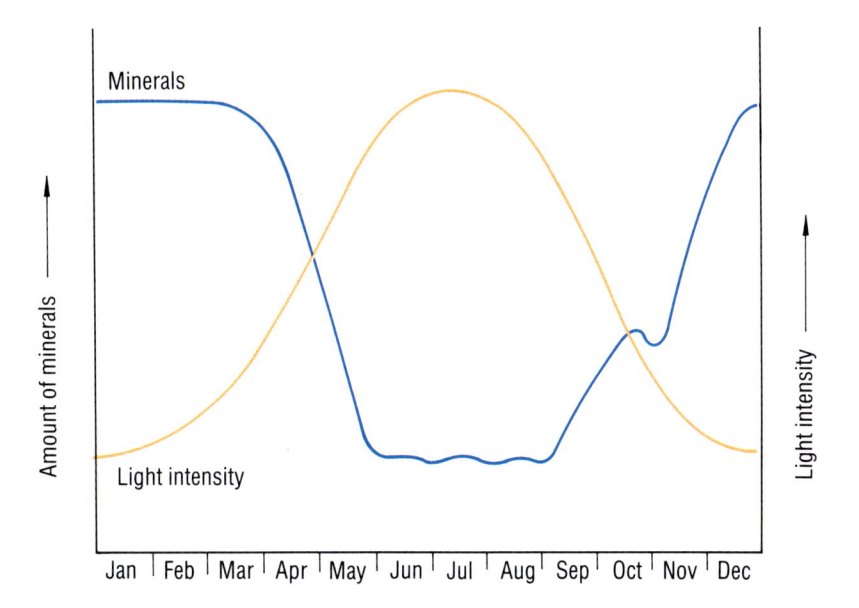

Figure 2.

1 Look at Figure 1. In what month are plankton numbers at their highest level?

2 What would the 'viz' be like at this time?

3 Look at Figure 2.
In January there is a good supply of minerals in the upper layers. What information in Figure 2 explains why the phytoplankton is not at a high level?

4 During March and April, mineral levels fall. What are the plants doing to cause this to happen?

5 What effect does the fall in mineral levels then seem to have on the amount of plankton?

6 In September and October, mineral levels in the surface waters rise again. What is happening to the sea which causes this?

7 What effect does the mineral rise have on plankton numbers?

8 During November and December the minerals rise still higher than in October. Why do phytoplankton levels not rise too?

9 There are two groups of months when 'viz' is good. When are these two periods?

10 Which of these groups of months will divers prefer to dive in?

1.3 Sampling trampling

One part of a football pitch usually looks much the same as another; it's a fairly uniform piece of vegetation. It's mostly grass with just a few other kinds of plant: daisy, dandelion and plantain, or 'ratstail'. A pitch also seems to change very little. It looks much the same one year as the next.

Even so it's surprising how easily the balance of plants in part of a field can be upset. At one school a new Science Block was built beside the football pitch. Quite soon people started taking a short cut home from the Science Block door at A, across the field and through a gap in the hedge at B, as shown in Figure 1.

Grass   Daisy   Ratstail plantain   Dandelion

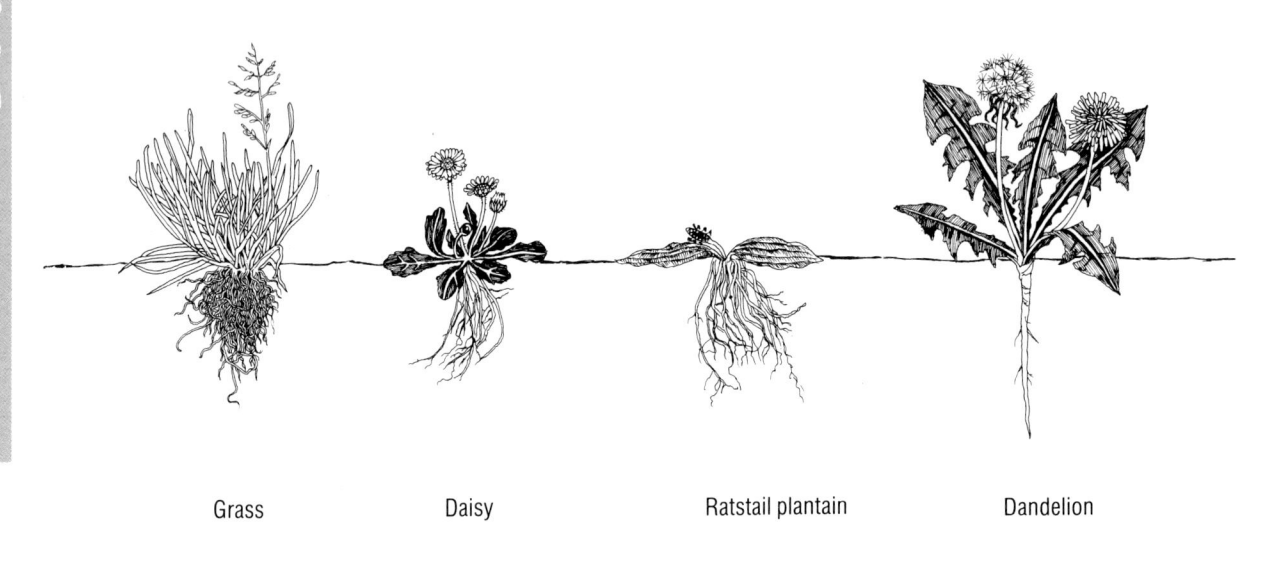

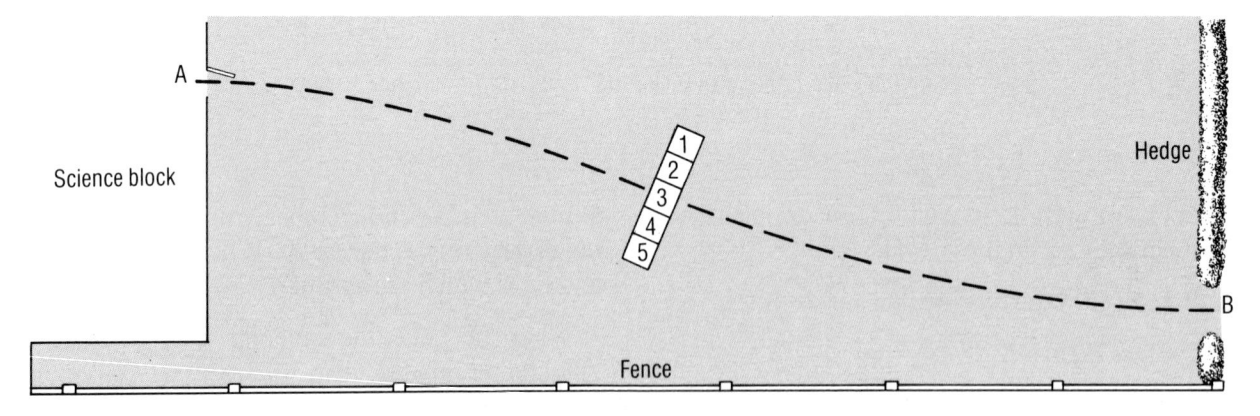

Figure 1. The short cut home.

The part people walked on soon began to look different. To find out the effect of people walking on the field, five survey areas were chosen for study, as shown in Figure 1. On each survey area a wire quadrat grid of 4 × 5 squares was laid. Each small square (10 cm × 10 cm) was carefully examined to see what was growing in it.

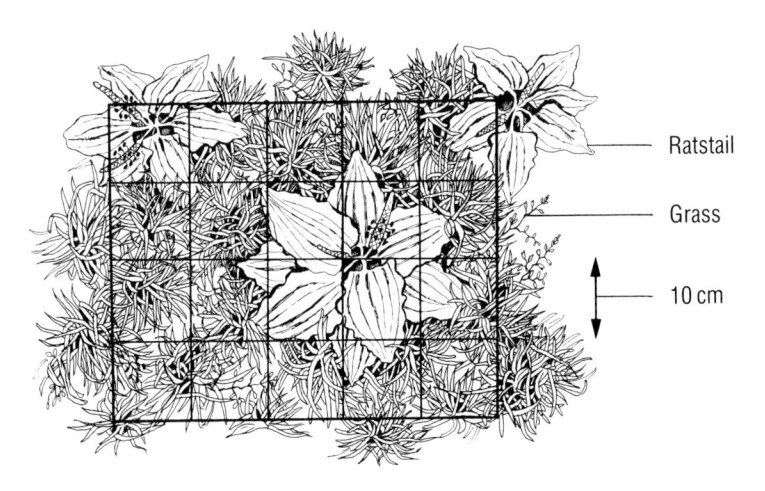

Figure 2. Area 2.

Any small square more than half covered by grass was counted as **all** grass – a 'grass square'. Any small square more than half covered by ratstail was counted as **all** ratstail – a 'ratstail square'.

The number of grass squares and ratstail squares was counted for each 4 × 5 square survey area, and the percentage of the survey area covered by each plant was worked out.

1 Look at Figure 2. How many small squares in area 2 are ratstail squares?

2 What percentage of area 2 is covered by ratstail?

3 Look at Figure 3. What percentage of area 5 is covered by grass?

4 Use the information given below to draw a bar chart showing the percentage of each of the five survey areas which is covered by **ratstail**. Note: you will have to use your answer to Question 2 to complete the table of information.

Area	5	4	3	2	1
Percentage cover	10	35	60	?	0

5 Look at the information for area 3.
a) What seems to be the effect on the grass cover in area 3 of people walking there?
b) What seems to be the effect on the ratstail cover in area 3 of people walking there?
c) Look at the pictures of a grass plant and of a ratstail plant. Suggest why trampling on them has different effects.

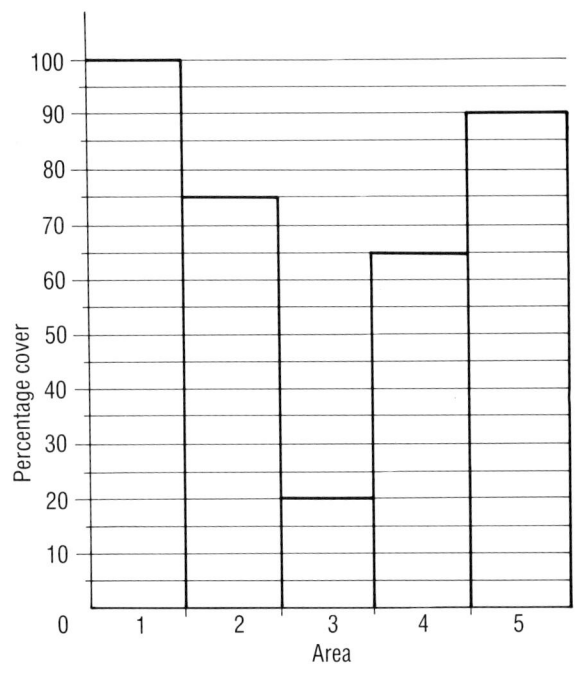

Figure 3. The bar chart shows the percentage of each of the five areas that is covered by grass.

6 a) What seems odd about the total figures for percentage cover in area 3?
b) Explain how this strange result is possible.

7 Plants in areas 2 and 4 are also affected by trampling.
a) Why are they affected?
b) Why is the effect less than in area 3?

8 This survey was a fairly simple one. What could you do to improve the accuracy of the measurements?

9 This survey concentrated on the region around the path. Describe what you could do to find out what the normal proportions of grass and plantains are over the whole pitch.

1.4 A rock pool

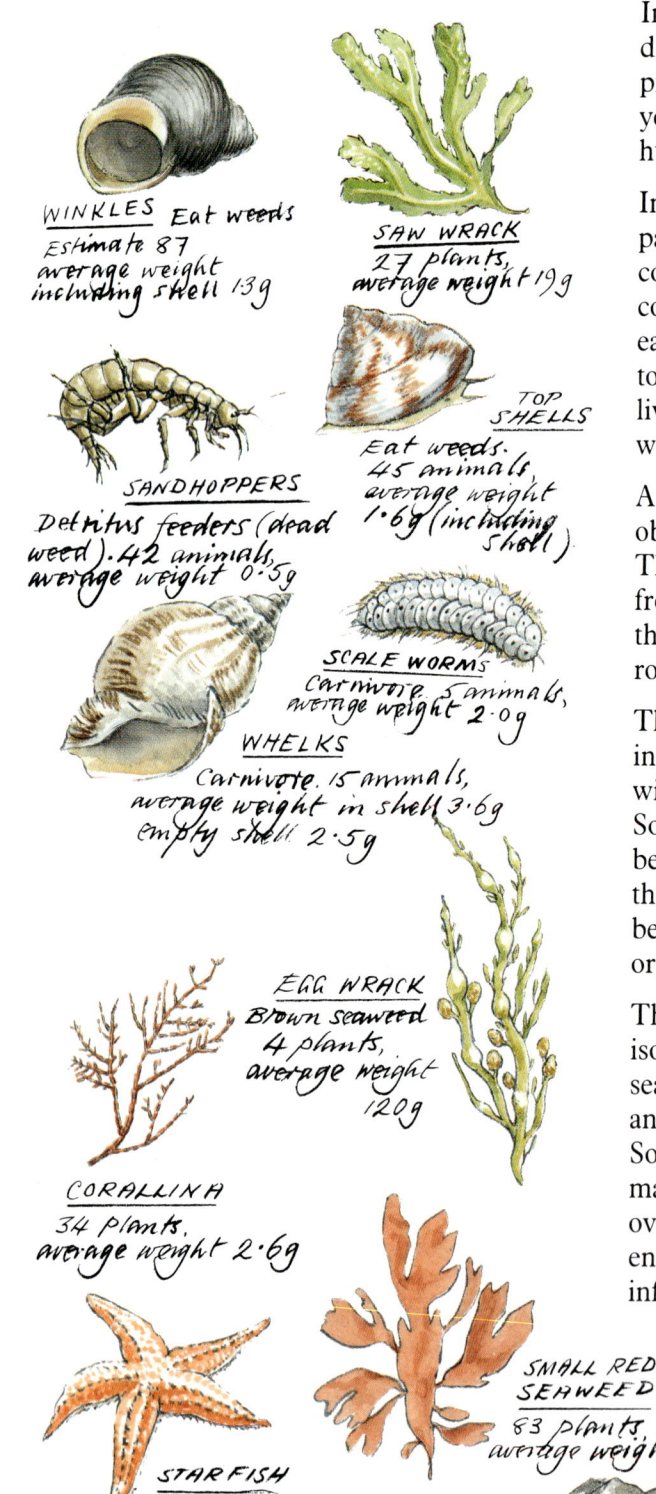

WINKLES Eat weeds. Estimate 87, average weight including shell 1.3g

SAW WRACK 27 plants, average weight 1.9g

SANDHOPPERS Detritus feeders (dead weed). 42 animals, average weight 0.5g

TOP SHELLS Eat weeds. 45 animals, average weight 1.6g (including shell)

SCALE WORMS Carnivore. 5 animals, average weight 2.0g

WHELKS Carnivore. 15 animals, average weight in shell 3.6g, empty shell 2.5g

EGG WRACK Brown seaweed. 4 plants, average weight 120g

CORALLINA 34 plants, average weight 2.6g

STARFISH Carnivore. 2 tiny ones, together weighing 2.8g

SMALL RED SEAWEED 83 plants, average weight 4.4g

ENCRUSTING WEED Not able to estimate

HERMIT CRABS Carnivores. Weights including shells 4.7, 6.4, 5.1, 6.5, 6.25, 8.6g

In a community of people the numbers in different occupation groups usually follow a predictable pattern. You would be surprised if you went to a village and found that out of five hundred people, two hundred were policemen.

In natural communities there are predictable patterns too. To see what these are you have to count the numbers of animals and plants in a community and try to find out how they relate to each other. Sometimes this is not easy as there are too many individuals to count or the community lives in such a large habitat that it is hard to know where to stop.

A seashore rock pool has the advantage that it is obvious, at low tide, where it begins and ends. The animals are trapped and cannot dash away from the biologist, but some are missed because they are well camouflaged. Others live under rocks and so may not be counted.

The pictures around this page show the information recorded from one rock pool. You will see that the information is not complete. Some is missing for organisms that would have been damaged or killed by being removed. Even the other information may be slightly inaccurate because the collector may not have noticed every organism.

The rock pool is not really a single completely isolated community. When the tide comes in the sea brings pieces of dead weed from other places and these can be eaten by the animals in the pool. Some of the animals found in the pool at low tide may move out of the pool at high tide, and feed over a wider area. Even so, a rock pool is small enough and isolated enough to provide useful information.

1 Copy the table below. Complete the first three columns about numbers of organisms. One organism at each level has been done for you. You add all the plants together to get 'total at this level'. Then you add all the herbivores, then all the carnivores.

2 Draw a bar chart to show the total numbers of organisms at each level.

3 Do you think this is a fair way of showing the amounts of each level of organism in the rock pool? Give a reason for your answer.

4 Calculate the average weight of a hermit crab. Do you think this is an underestimate or an overestimate of the real weight of living crab? Why?

5 Complete the weights part of the table. (Weight of saw wrack = 27 plants × 19 g average weight = 513 g.)

6 a) Draw a bar chart to show the total weights of organisms at each level.
b) How is it different from your first bar chart?

Level	Name	Numbers		Weights = biomass	
		in group	Total at level	One organism × number	of group	Total at level
Plants (= producers)	Saw wrack	27		19 × 27	513	
Herbivores and detritus feeders (= first consumers)	Winkles	87		1.3 × 87	113.1	
Carnivores (= second consumers)	Whelks	15		3.6 × 15	54	

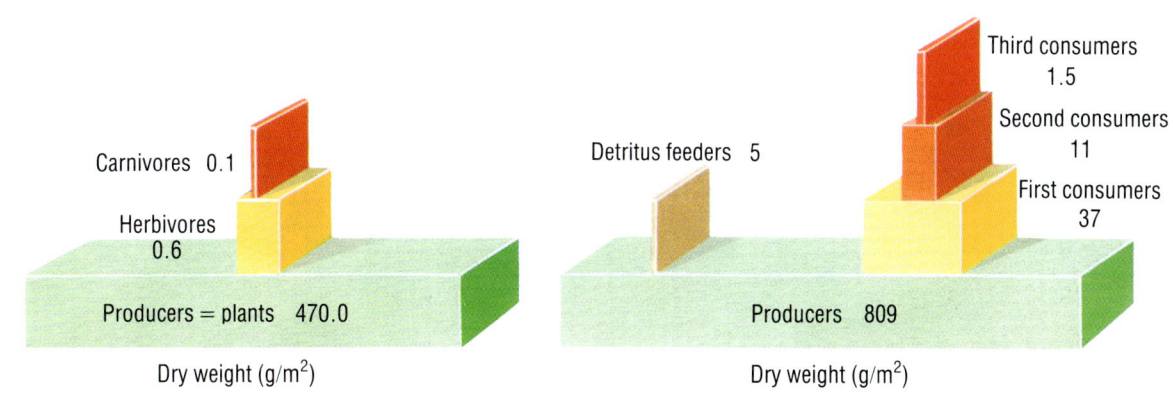

Figure 1. Pyramid of biomass for an established meadow community.
Carnivores 0.1
Herbivores 0.6
Producers = plants 470.0
Dry weight (g/m²)

Figure 2. Pyramid of biomass for a river community.
Third consumers 1.5
Second consumers 11
First consumers 37
Detritus feeders 5
Producers 809
Dry weight (g/m²)

7 What point about the rock pool community is being made in the last paragraph opposite?

Biologists have collected information about many communities. The diagrams in Figures 1 and 2 show how they are often displayed. Plants are at the bottom and carnivores are at the top.

8 Do the diagrams in Figures 1 and 2 show roughly the same proportions of plants (producers), herbivores and carnivores as the rock pool figures?

9 How do your answers to Questions 4 and 7 help to explain any difference?

1.5 Tides and living conditions

Every hour of every day around the coast of Britain, the sea level is changing. These changes in sea level, or tides, make the zone where the land meets the sea a special one. Temperature, available water and saltiness may change dramatically every few hours.

Animals and plants which can survive such frequent changes in environmental conditions are obviously rather special. They will vary in their ability to survive on the seashore. Different parts of the seashore will have different conditions too. The upper shore will only be under water for one or two hours each day, while the lower shore will be under water almost all the time. It will only be uncovered for an hour or two each day.

What effect does all this have on the distribution of plants and animals on the seashore? Here is how one group of people studied an area of rocky seashore, and what they discovered about where the different seaweeds grow.

At low tide, one team laid out a measuring tape from high tide mark to the water's edge. They measured and recorded the horizontal distance and vertical drop every 0.5 m along the tape. Later they made an accurate scale drawing of the profile of the shore where the tape was laid out (Figure 1).

This made it possible to take any point along the tape and find its vertical height above low water.

Figure 1. Shore profile.

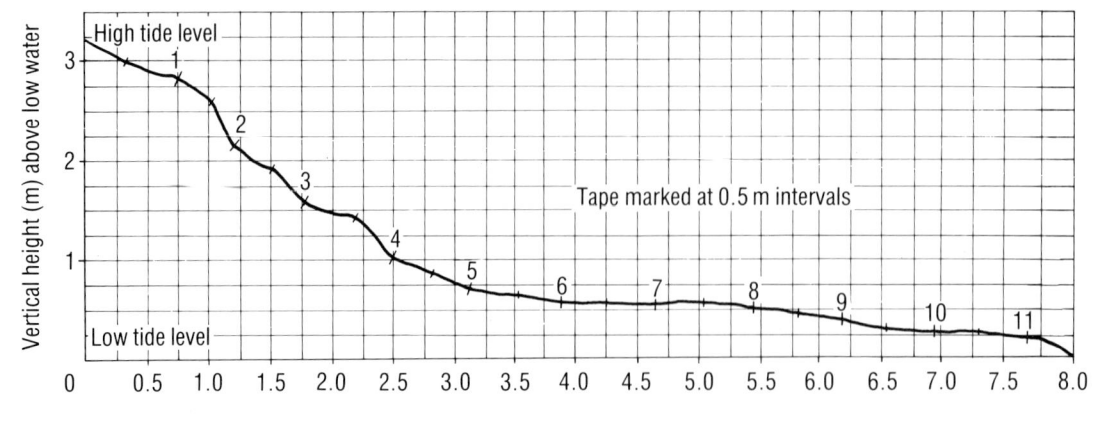

Another team looked carefully at a narrow band on either side of the tape, and identified some of the seaweeds growing there, noting where they started and finished on the tape. Their results are given in Table 1.

They then used the shore profile to find the vertical heights of the points on the tape, and began to draw up Table 2.

The last stage was to convert the information in Table 2 into a diagram like Figure 2, using a separate vertical line for each seaweed.

Table 2

Seaweed species	Where found (*vertical height* above low water)	
	Highest point	Lowest point
Serrated wrack		
Kelp		
Knotted wrack		
Spiral wrack		
Channelled wrack	3.0 m	2.25 m
Bladder wrack		

Table 1

Seaweed species	Where found *along tape*	
	Highest point	Lowest point
Serrated wrack	8.0 m	Below water
Kelp	11.0 m	Below water
Knotted wrack	3.0 m	8.5 m
Spiral wrack	1.5 m	3.5 m
Channelled wrack	0.5 m	2.0 m
Bladder wrack	2.5 m	9.0 m

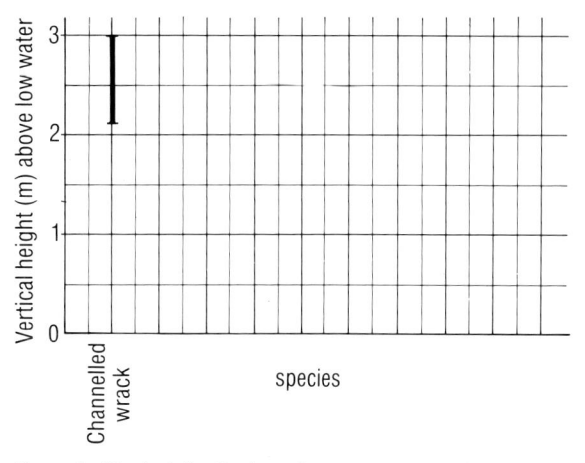

Figure 2. Vertical distribution of common seaweeds.

Question 1 takes you through the steps involved in making a diagram to show the vertical distribution of seaweeds.

1 a) Copy and complete Table 2 using the information in Figure 1.
b) Write a list of the species of seaweed in order. Start with the species which grows highest up the shore, then the next highest, and so on down to the lowest.
c) Copy Figure 2 on to a piece of graph paper. Using your completed Table 2, add vertical lines to represent the other kinds of seaweeds. Put them in the same order as in your list for Question 1b).

Seaweeds common on rocky shores.

2 Describe the pattern of distribution of each of the seaweeds on this shore.

3 Which seaweed seems least able to tolerate being out of the water?

4 Describe the physical conditions in which the channelled wrack is living, and the problems that it faces as a result.

1.6 Stocking a tropical aquarium

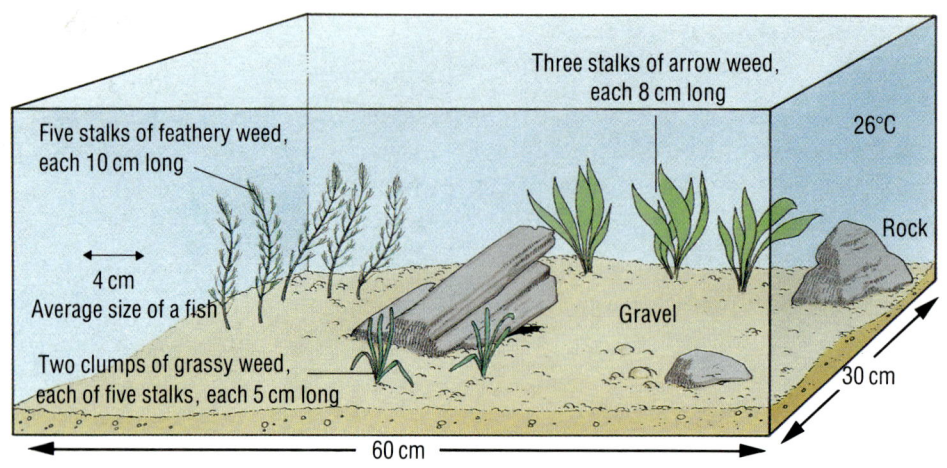

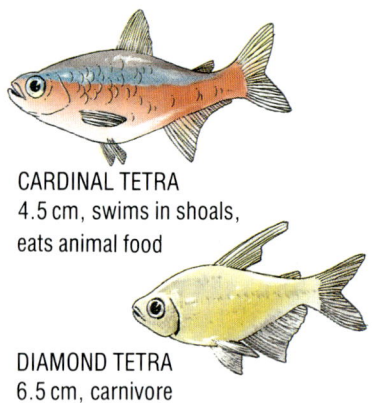

Aquarium diagram labels:
- Five stalks of feathery weed, each 10 cm long
- Three stalks of arrow weed, each 8 cm long
- 26 °C
- Rock
- 4 cm Average size of a fish
- Gravel
- Two clumps of grassy weed, each of five stalks, each 5 cm long
- 30 cm
- 60 cm

Mid-water fish

CARDINAL TETRA
4.5 cm, swims in shoals, eats animal food

DIAMOND TETRA
6.5 cm, carnivore

HARLEQUIN BARB
4.5 cm, best in shoals, carnivore

GUPPY
3 cm, eats plants and animals

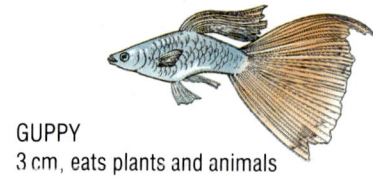

Imagine that you have to set up the tank in the picture. The gravel and rocks were put in first and then the water was added. It has been left to settle and to reach the right temperature. The habitat is ready. The heater, lights and filter pump are working correctly. You have chosen and planted the greenery. None of it has died, so everything is ready for the fish.

How many fish can you put in and what kinds should they be? In a *crowded* tank fish may fight for space to swim in or corners to hide in. If one becomes diseased the illness may spread very quickly to the other fish. If you choose *too few* fish the aquarium will look dull and empty.

Fish need the oxygen that is dissolved in the water. The oxygen gets into the water through its surface. Aquarium experts say that every centimetre length of fish needs 30 cm^2 of surface area of tank. So the tank in the picture can hold 20 fish if they are all 3 cm long but only 10 fish if each is 6 cm long.

Each type of fish chooses to live in a particular part of the tank. Usually aquarium keepers put in more than half of the total number as middle swimmers, and then choose some that will stay near the surface and a few that are bottom feeders.

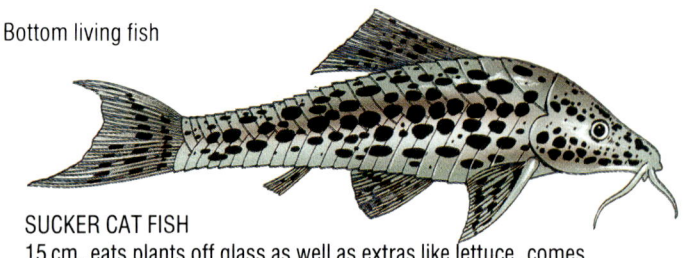

Bottom living fish

SUCKER CAT FISH
15 cm, eats plants off glass as well as extras like lettuce, comes out at night, will live on its own

LEOPARD CAT FISH
6 cm, eats plants and dead material, active in the day time, need to be at least two together

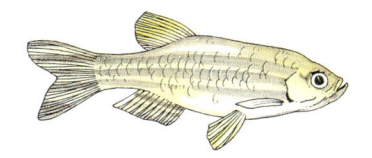

ZEBRA DARIO
5 cm, fast swimmer, insect feeder

BLACK WINGED HATCHET FISH
4.5 cm, often jumps out of tank,
loves small insects to eat

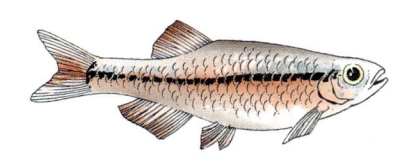

WHITE CLOUD MOUNTAIN MINNOW
4.5 cm, usually very active,
feeds on animals on surface

Surface fish

1 This tank can hold 60 cm as its total length of fish.
a) Work on scrap paper. Choose the types and numbers of fish for your tank. Check that their total length is not more than 60 cm.
b) Continue in your normal note book. Copy the table, and complete the first two columns using your choice of fish.

2 Calculate the values needed to complete the rest of the table. Use the pictures to check the feeding habits of the fish.

3 Plot bar charts to show the *numbers* of:
a) plants.
b) plant-eating animals (herbivores), including those eating dead material.
c) omnivores (eat plants and animals).
d) carnivores (eat animals).

4 Calculate what length of fish could be kept in a tank of 60 cm × 60 cm surface area.

	Organism	No.	Total length (cm)	Feeding habits
Plants	Feathery weed	5	5 × 10 = 50	–
	Arrow weed	3		–
	Grassy weed			–
Fish				

5 The ↔ on the tank shows the size of a 4 cm fish.
a) Do you think that your bar charts show the *amounts* of each group clearly?
b) Repeat the bar charts using total lengths in each group instead of numbers.
c) Do you think that this chart shows the amounts of the groups in a better way?
d) Do you think that any other measurement would make an even fairer comparison? If so, what is it?

6 a) Does your aquarium community show the proportions of carnivores that you expected? (Clue: pyramid of numbers.)
b) A natural tropical pond survives for years without human assistance but you will have to feed your tank. What information on your charts suggests why this is so?

7 This fish was in a tank in a shop and had no label. Compare its shape with those of the other fish, and suggest the level in the tank it will live at. Say why you chose this group.

8 Angel fish are mid-water carnivores that can grow up to 15 cm long. Why would they be a bad choice if you had guppies in the tank already?

BIOSPHERE

1.7 The web

THE WEB

The spider's web, stretched between the twigs of the sycamore tree, trembled gently in the light breeze. The spider hung motionless at the centre of the web, legs stretched out fore and aft. Waiting!

The strands of web furthest from the centre were festooned with 'parcels' of various sizes – bundles of gossamer spun by the spider and attached to the web. Closer inspection showed that at the centre of each bundle were the remains of an insect, and in many cases it was possible to tell from protruding wings or legs what kind of insect had been trapped in the web, paralysed by a bite from the spider, and wrapped in silk to be stored.

Most of the 'larder' consisted of sycamore greenfly, which had fed on the leaf sap as nymphs, moulting and growing, until, at the final moult, they became winged adults.

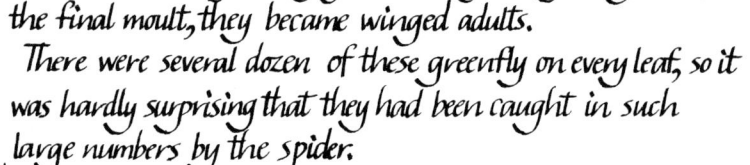

There were several dozen of these greenfly on every leaf, so it was hardly surprising that they had been caught in such large numbers by the spider.

One or two of the bundles contained adult Braconid wasps – tiny insects whose larvae are parasitic on greenfly.

The largest bundle showed the large compound eyes, short antennae and yellow and black stripes of a hover-fly, which had just visited the sycamore tree to lay its eggs, only to blunder into the spider's web. The eggs which were laid would hatch into legless maggot-like larvae, which would feed on the greenfly while roaming around the twigs and leaves of the tree, despite their lack of legs.

A ray of sunlight caught in the web, making its threads glisten for a few seconds.

A willow-warbler, foraging among the branches, noticed the web, and added the spider to the beakful of caterpillars and greenfly it had already collected from the young leaves near the ends of the twigs.

The bird flew off into the wood in the direction of the nest, where its young brood were consuming greater amounts of insects every day.

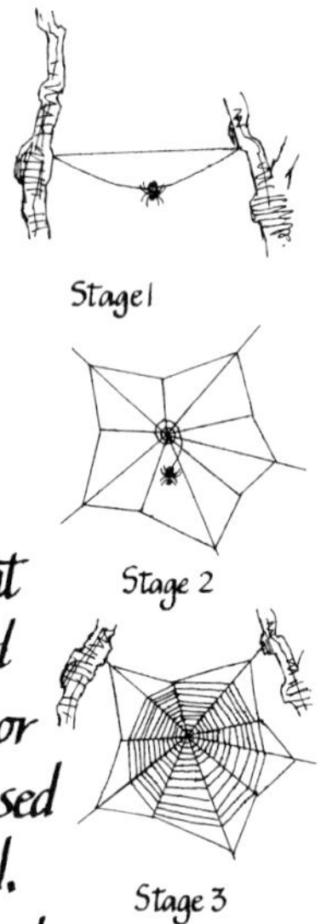

Web showing arrangement of 'bundles'

Epeira diademata: garden spider

male

female

Detail of hover-fly bundle

Stage 1

Stage 2

Stage 3

Stages in web-building

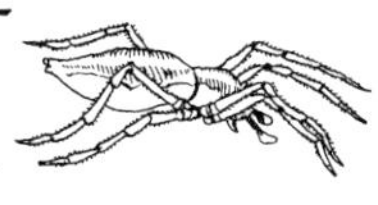

Pisaura: hunting spider

1 Make a list of all the organisms mentioned and what each one eats. (Do not count 'insects' as a separate group, since many of the organisms are different kinds of insect.)

2 Use this information to draw a food web.

1.8 Pioneers

How large a population grows depends on how well the animals' environment supplies their needs. Animals need food to eat, fresh air and water. They need a chance to mate and space for the young to grow. Shortage of any of these essentials will keep down the number of animals. Predators will lower the numbers still further.

Some idea of the maximum number an area can support can be seen when a few pioneer individuals move into a new and previously unpopulated area, where there is little or no problem with predators.

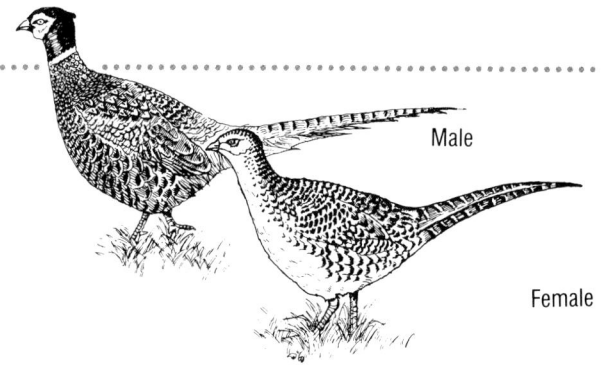

A pair of ring-necked pheasants.

In 1937 two male and six female ring-necked pheasants were set free on the tiny Protection Island off the coast of Washington state, USA. The number of pheasants on the island was counted each spring and autumn for seven years.

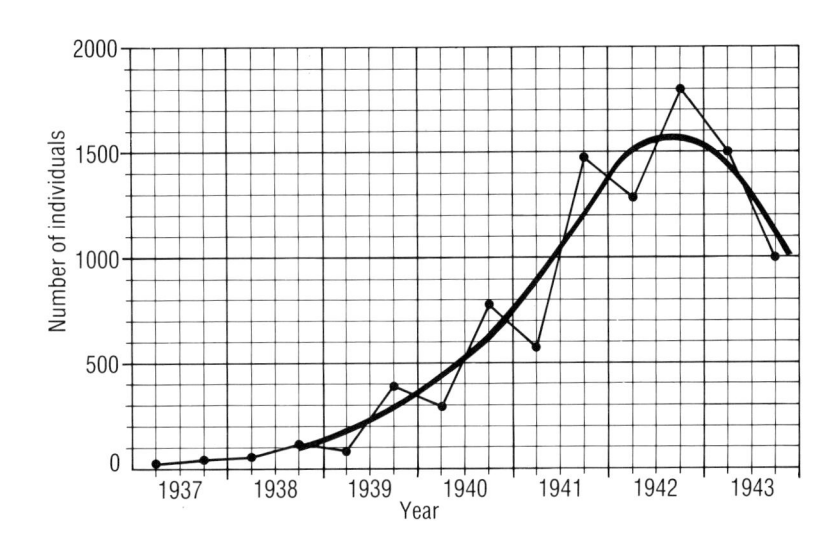

The growth of the pheasant population.

The graph shows what happened. The thin straight lines join the numbers from the spring and autumn counts. The heavy line shows the average numbers for each year.

1 Copy the table below and complete it to show the numbers of pheasants found at the spring count each year.

Year	1937	1938	1939	1940	1941	1942	1943
Number	8	20					

2 From the information on the graph, write sentences to say what happened to the number of pheasants in the year from spring 1940 to spring 1941.

3 Suggest a reason for the change in numbers between the autumn count and the count made the next spring.

4 a) In which year was the average population growing *fastest*?
b) What feature of the graph tells you this?

5 The population increase in 1942 was slower than in earlier years. Suggest *two* factors which might be limiting the rise in population.

6 This population survey was carried out on an island. In what ways does this make the problem easier to study?

7 Unfortunately, the survey was interrupted in 1943 when the island was made a base for US soldiers. Suggest a probable reason for the sudden fall in the number of pheasants.

1.9 Sharing out the energy

The sun shines on the earth. Plants turn a small amount of the light energy into chemical energy. They can store it as food which they use themselves and they can be eaten. As food provides energy, a food web also shows how energy is moved about between the members of the community.

No animal deliberately gets fat to make a good meal for another animal. Animals use the food that they take in for themselves.

One of the most famous food web studies was carried out in Wytham Wood in Oxfordshire.

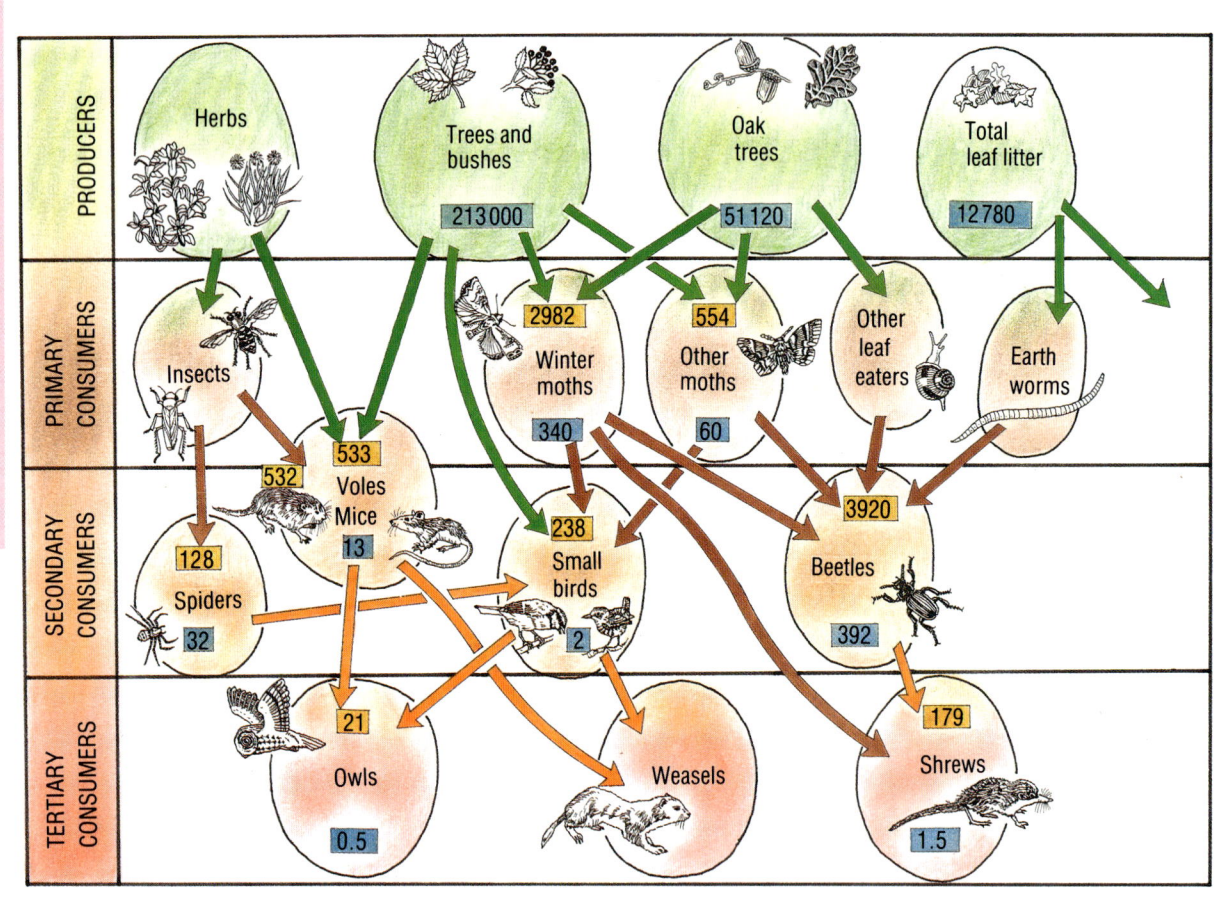

The diagram above is roughly based on the results from Wytham Wood.

Figure 1.
Energy figures for a woodland community.
The numbers are megajoules/hectare/year.

Biologists estimated the numbers of the different kinds of trees in the area and calculated the energy value of the food available to the herbivores. They then estimated the numbers of most of the kinds of animals there, and observed what food each animal ate. They studied animals' eating habits and estimated how much each group would eat in a year. It was a very detailed and time-consuming project. Even when they were finished the figures were not complete.

The numbers (on orange) above each group show the energy in the food it takes in, and the numbers (on blue) below show what that group provides to the animals further along the food chain.

For example, the whole spider population takes in 128 MJ of energy in food in one year. It provides 32 MJ of 'new spider' that could be eaten by predators or could be decomposed if the spiders died without being eaten.

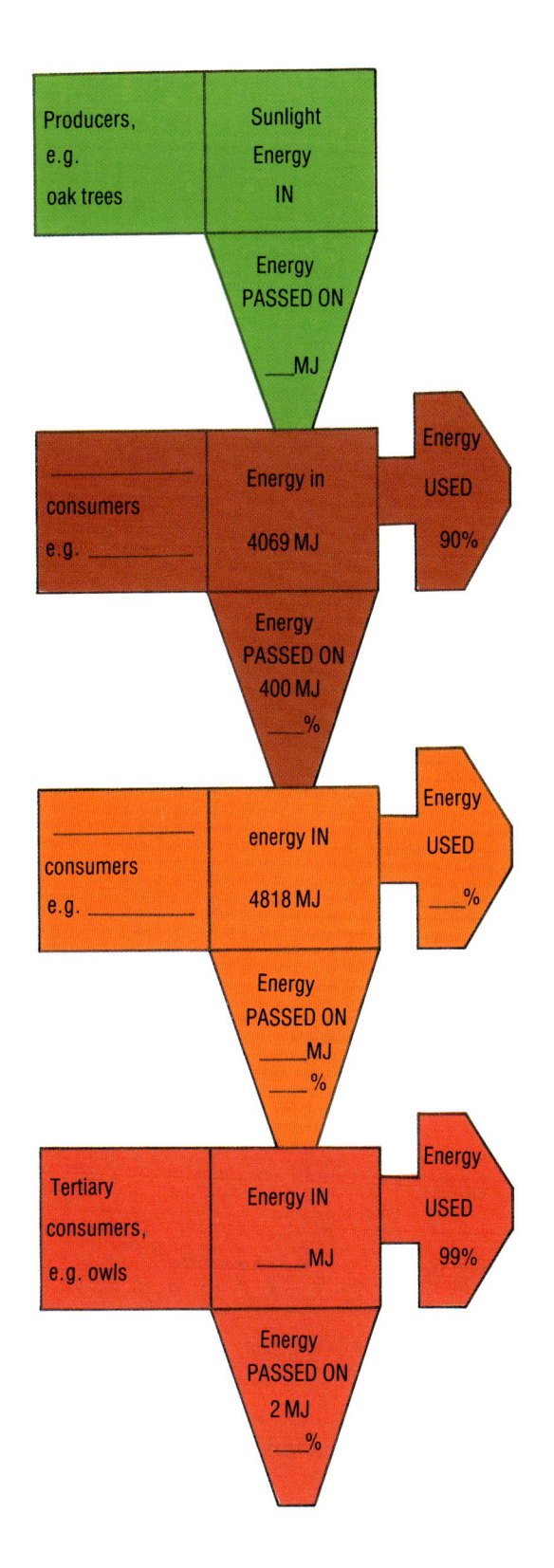

Figure 2. Summary of energy transfer in a woodland community.

1 Study Figure 1 carefully and check that you can understand the numbers.
a) How much energy is taken in by the beetles?
b) How much energy can beetles provide to other animals?
c) What percentage of what they take in do beetles pass on to others?
d) What percentage of the food that they take in is used by the beetles?
e) What do the beetles do with the energy that they use? (If you have no idea look at 'Input = output?' on page 61.)

The next questions will help you to complete a summary diagram.

2 Copy Figure 2, but draw it larger.

3 Write *primary* and *secondary* in the correct boxes.

4 Add up and put into the correct place in your diagram these figures:
a) total energy passed on by plants.
b) total energy passed on by secondary consumers.

5 Calculate and write in the missing values for:
a) energy in.
b) percentage passed on.
c) percentage used.

6 Some books say that '10% of the energy is passed from one group of consumers to the next'. Calculate from Figure 1 what percentage **a)** spiders and **b)** small birds are passing on. Comment on the above statement.

7 Why do you think energy figures are not available for some parts of the food web?

8 It may well surprise you that your summary diagram shows the secondary consumers taking in more energy than the primary consumers passed on. Use Figure 1 to explain this.

9 Suggest two reasons why the tertiary consumers in this food web use such a very high percentage of the energy they take in.

10 'Eating less meat and more vegetable products is a better way to feed the world'. How do the calculations that you made support this statement?

1.10 Competition for survival

'Only the strong survive'
'Nature red in tooth and claw'

These phrases bring to mind lions stalking zebra on the African plains, but an equally deadly struggle for survival can take place in a tiny pond.

When the water flea (*Daphnia*) and the rotifer shown on the right are together they compete for the same food: single-celled green algae, bacteria and the remains of dead organisms.

An experiment was set up, as shown in Figure 1, to study the numbers of these two species as they compete for food. Fresh single-celled algae, for food, were added daily.

The competitors.

When both types of animal were present (flask 3) the rotifers began to look starved and transparent after 10 days.

Figure 1. Flasks and animals.

Flask 1 — Rotifers alone
Flask 2 — Daphnia alone
Flask 3 — Rotifers + Daphnia

These results suggest that rotifers should have died out by now, but in real ponds there are many reasons why rotifers outnumber water fleas. When there is plenty of food the rotifers may simply multiply faster. Rotifers are much smaller than water fleas so they may be able to feed in places water fleas cannot reach, and fish may not be able to see them to catch them, although they can see water fleas.

- ■ Rotifers alone (flask 1)
- ● Daphnia alone (flask 2)
- □ Rotifers ⎫ (flask 3)
- ○ Daphnia ⎭

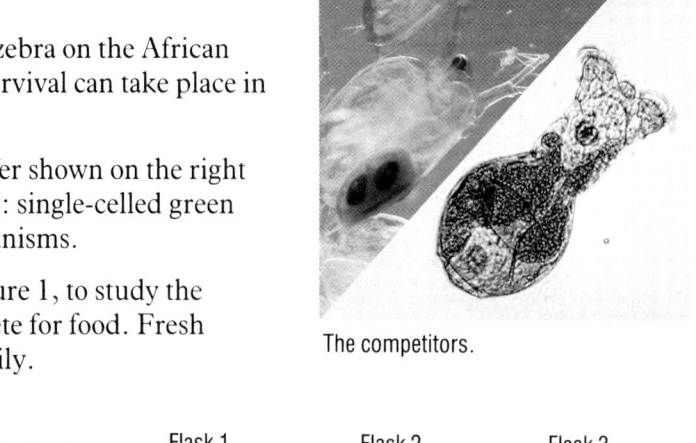

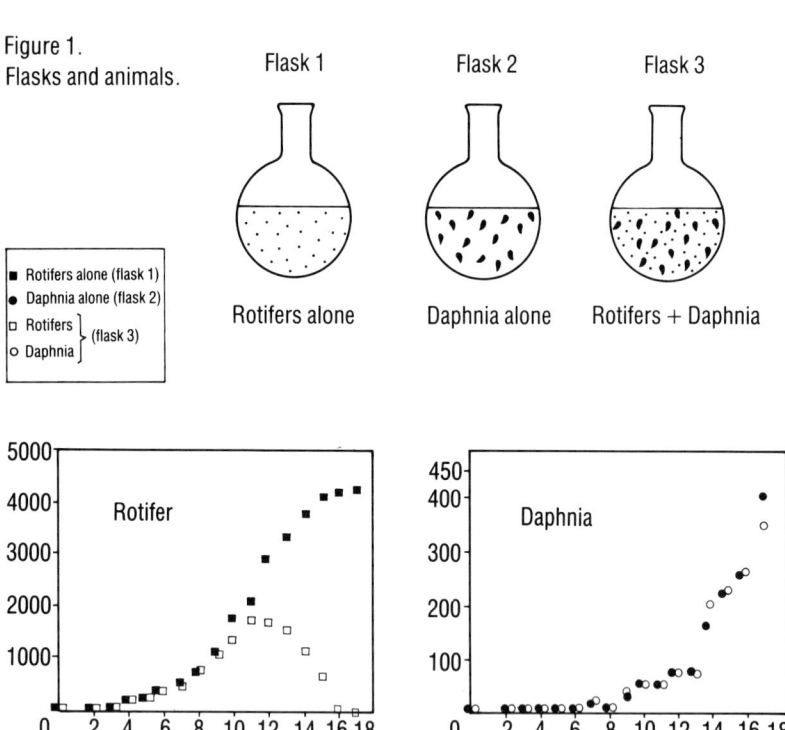

Figure 2. Changes in population sizes over a 17-day period.

1 Describe the changes in numbers over the 17 days of the experiment for:
a) 'rotifers alone' (flask 1).
b) 'water fleas alone' (flask 2).

2 Why is it necessary to have these two single-species flasks (1 and 2) when the point of the experiment is to find out about competition between the two species?

3 Which of the flasks are controls?

4 Compare the numbers of water fleas alone (flask 2) with the numbers of water fleas when with rotifers (flask 3).

5 What happens to the numbers of rotifers when water fleas and rotifers are together in flask 3?

6 For what could water fleas and rotifers be competing in flask 3?

7 Explain why this experiment does not represent a natural freshwater environment.

1.11 How many seeds should I sow?

Seed packets tell us how far apart to plant the seeds. Too far apart and there will be too much bare ground so the garden will not look as attractive. Too close together and the plants will not grow as well, and we may get tall spindly plants with fewer flowers.

Plants that are too close together in the vegetable garden will have to compete with each other for light, water and minerals. The result will be a poorer crop yield. If the plants are too far apart, a lot of growing space is wasted and competition with weeds may reduce the crop yield. Growers must therefore space their plants to make the best use of the land.

In some parts of the world, sunflowers are grown as a commercial crop. Many health foods are made from sunflower seeds and sunflower oil has become very popular for cooking since it contains mainly polyunsaturated fats. Sunflower oil is also used for making margarine.

Some crop research scientists sowed different numbers of sunflower seeds on equal-sized plots of land. At harvest-time, they measured the amount of seed produced in two ways. They counted how many seeds came from each flower-head, and they measured the total weight of seeds from each plot. Their results are shown in Tables 1 and 2.

Table 1 Effect of seed sowing on numbers of seeds produced on each sunflower head

No. of seeds sown per m^2	10	50	100	200	700	2500
No. of seeds per head	1800	900	500	200	100	10

Table 2 Effect of seed sowing on weight of seeds produced

No. of seeds sown per m^2	50	100	200	600	2500
Seed yield (kg/m^2)	2.9	2.8	4.0	3.0	1.6

1 Draw graphs from Tables 1 and 2. (You will need to use a long horizontal scale.)

2 What are the effects of sowing very large numbers of seeds per square metre on:
a) numbers of seeds per head?
b) total seed yield (kg/m^2)?

3 What factors could have caused these effects?

4 What number of seeds per square metre would you recommend a farmer to sow to give him the maximum crop (i.e. maximum total seed yield)?

1.12 Effects of acidity

As many city dwellers, especially those with bronchitis, will know, coal and oil burning releases irritating sulphur dioxide gas into the atmosphere. Sulphur dioxide gas in the air dissolves in rain water. So do oxides of nitrogen, which are put into the air by power stations and car exhausts. These pollutants increase the acidity of rain enough to have serious effects on the environment.

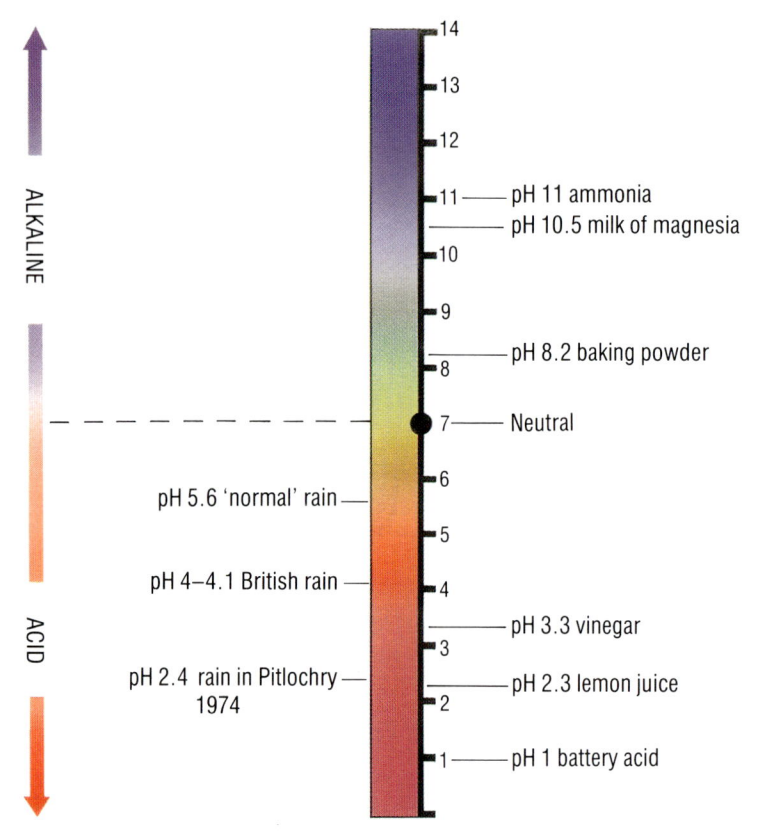

Figure 1. Acidity and alkalinity scale.

- pH 11 ammonia
- pH 10.5 milk of magnesia
- pH 8.2 baking powder
- 7 Neutral
- pH 5.6 'normal' rain
- pH 4–4.1 British rain
- pH 3.3 vinegar
- pH 2.4 rain in Pitlochry 1974
- pH 2.3 lemon juice
- pH 1 battery acid

Damaged trees, possibly caused by acid rain.

Natural, unpolluted rain is not neutral. Carbon dioxide from the atmosphere dissolves in it and makes it slightly acid. When this rain lands, its normal acidity is usually neutralized by the soil and the minerals in lakes and rivers. If rain is more acid than normal it makes the soil more acid, and it also runs off the land into streams, rivers and lakes, making them acid too. Limestone, in the ground, can usually neutralize some of the acid, so that lake and stream habitats are not always as acid as the rain which falls on them. In areas with little limestone the damage being done to aquatic ecosystems can be very serious. As Figure 2 shows, many crustaceans are affected as soon as the pH falls below 6.0. The managers of trout fisheries have blamed acid rain for fish deaths. In Scandinavia, ecologists report that many lakes are completely dead.

1 Use Figures 1 and 2 together to answer these questions.
a) What living organisms are likely to be found in water that is as acid as British rain?
b) What would you expect to find living in water with the same pH as 'normal' rain?
c) How does the most acid rain, recorded at Pitlochry in 1974, compare with household acids?

| pH | 7.5 | 7.0 | 6.5 | 6.0 | 5.5 | 5.0 | 4.5 | 4.0 | 3.5 |

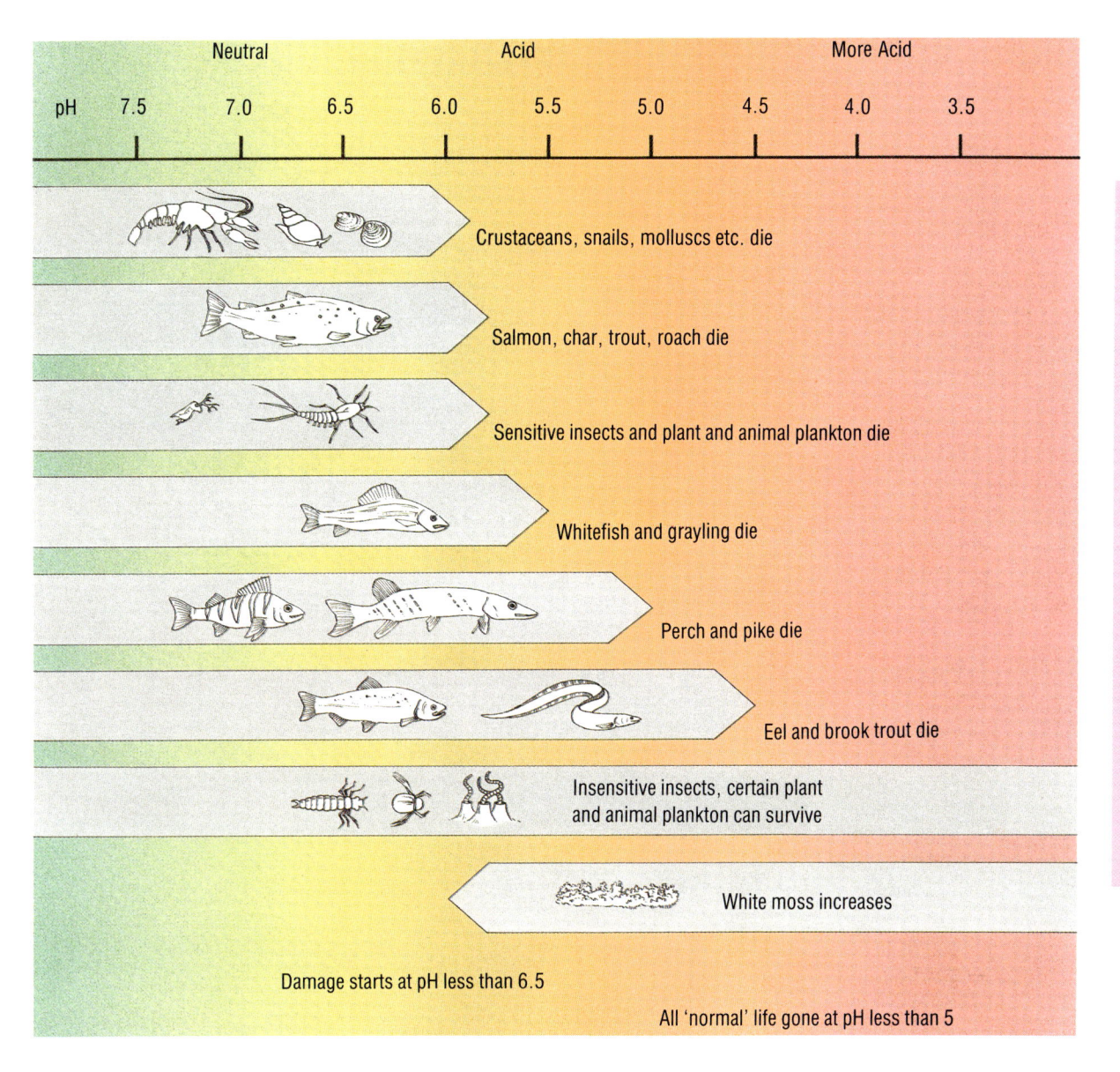

Neutral — Acid — More Acid

- Crustaceans, snails, molluscs etc. die
- Salmon, char, trout, roach die
- Sensitive insects and plant and animal plankton die
- Whitefish and grayling die
- Perch and pike die
- Eel and brook trout die
- Insensitive insects, certain plant and animal plankton can survive
- White moss increases

Damage starts at pH less than 6.5

All 'normal' life gone at pH less than 5

Figure 2. Susceptibility of organisms to acid.

Acid rain not only affects water environments, but it also falls on plants and the soil. Acid water in the soil may damage plants by making them take up abnormal amounts of minerals, in particular metals like aluminium. Acid rain is blamed for causing much damage to trees, especially conifers.

In Sweden many people draw their water from wells which are filled by rainwater trickling through the soil. Householders receiving their water through copper pipes have had problems with green tap water. This is caused by copper dissolving in the very acid well water. Copper can be poisonous. The World Health Organization recommends that drinking water should not contain more than 0.05 mg of copper per litre. Acid rain is believed to have been the cause of copper levels 10 times higher than this. Such levels of copper are suspected of causing diarrhoea in children. High levels of aluminium have also been recorded. For this reason, hospitals in Sweden now check the pH and dissolved metal content of their water supplies before using it for patients on kidney machines. Aluminium can kill people who have damaged kidneys.

2 Identify three main themes from these two pages.

1.13 Cause for complaint

The Forth River Purification Board is responsible for monitoring pollution in the River Forth. It keeps a record of complaints received from the public about the state of the river and its tributaries. Some of the complaints may be serious. Others may be about something which is an eyesore but is not very harmful to the ecosystem. Small animals may even find human throwaways quite useful sometimes!

The serious complaints, however, usually concern chemicals, oil or sewage. Something in the water may kill fish. You have probably seen pictures of 'oiled' seabirds on the news so it should not surprise you that oil is harmful to other organisms. You may also have seen reports about holiday beaches being polluted by sewage. The monitoring of such beaches is done to see if they meet EEC standards of hygiene.

Table 1 Some complaints to the Forth River Board, 1977–1984

Complaint	77	78	79	80	81	82	83	84
Oil	97	114	102	128	80	135	83	88
Sewage and sewage sludge	92	97	76	74	94	93	81	95
Industrial waste discharge	53	46	85	70	43	40	36	58
Farm waste	42	39			38	25	32	34
Tipping and rubbish	23	23			16	31	32	34
Inert solids (e.g. car in river)	19	14	–	2	1	2	1	2
Fish mortalities	17	26	32	19	19	29	30	16
Natural pollution	2	1	4	2	4	2	–	2
Dead animals in water	2	–	5	2	1	6	2	1
Spillage by road tanker (not oil)	2	2	2	–	–	1	–	1
Foam in river	–	6	7	4	3	6	5	13
Silage liquor	–	–	5	16	23	14	21	10
Discolouration	6	9	8	34	21	21	17	22
Total complaints (includes categories not listed above)	391	428	415	434	401	463	388	474

The table shows some of the complaints investigated by the Forth River Purification Board over a number of years. You can see that sewage and oil are by no means the only forms of pollution.

1 Calculate the average numbers of oil pollution complaints in the three-year periods:
a) 1977–1979.
b) 1982–1984.

2 What percentages of the total complaints were about sewage and sewage sludge in:
a) 1977?
b) 1984?

3 Use the picture and table to name two ways in which farming can be a cause of water pollution.

4 Is farming more or less polluting than industry according to these figures? Give reasons for your answer.

5 Do you think that the amount of pollution in the River Forth has increased or decreased over the years shown on the table? Give reasons for your answer.

6 Do you think that complaints by members of the public to the Forth River Purification Board provide a good measure of sources of pollution? List some other measures that might be possible.

7 If there was discoloration of the water at point X on the map below, what investigations could you make?

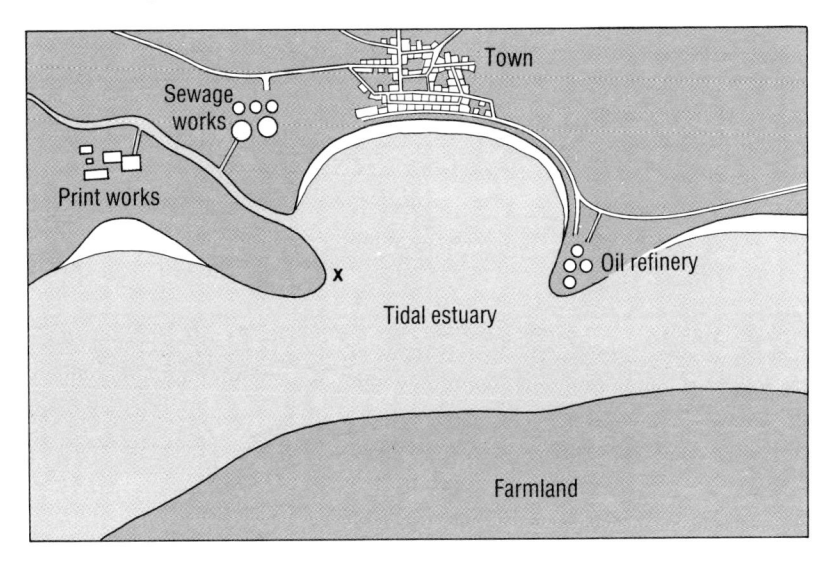

2.1 Uses of plants

PLANTS

- Animal feed (HAY)
- Apples, bananas, tomatoes
- Cane chair
- CIGARETTES
- Cinchona bark / MALARIA TABLETS
- Coleus
- CORN FLAKES
- Cotton
- Cyclamen
- Foxglove / Digitalis / HEART PILLS
- Grass pitch and wooden goal posts
- Henna / HAIR DYE
- Herbaceous border
- Hockey stick
- Indigo (dye)
- Jasmine / Perfume
- Lavender / fine Soap
- Flax / Linen
- Match sticks / BLUEBELL
- Oak table
- Oatmeal face pack

24

The pictures on these two pages show some uses of plants. They are arranged in alphabetical order. You can probably think of many other ways in which plants are used, for example, for woad in Ancient Britain, or palm leaf thatch and grass skirts, or semolina pudding.

1 Study the pictures and decide on at least five main group names into which you could sort them. (You are allowed to have a small 'Miscellaneous' group.)

2 Make a table with the names of your groups as column headings. Work through the pictures writing the title of each into a column.

3 Draw a pie chart to show the distribution of plant uses between your columns. (Hint: there are 33 pictures. 3 × 33 = 99. This is near enough to 100 for you to use 3 times your total for a column as a percentage of the whole.)

4 Think of plants, and plant products, that you use daily. Do you think that the numbers in each of your columns give a fair idea of real everyday use of each category? Give a reason for your answer.

5 Copy the diagram below.

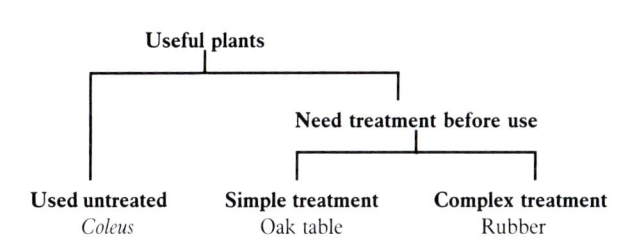

```
                    Useful plants
                  ┌──────┴──────┐
                         Need treatment before use
                         ┌───────┴───────┐
Used untreated      Simple treatment    Complex treatment
   Coleus              Oak table             Rubber
```

a) Look through your columns and the pictures. Write the names of the pictures that show plants being used untreated under the correct part of the diagram. The first one has been done for you.

b) Divide the rest into ones which need little treatment and those which need a complex extraction process. Again the first ones have been done for you.

2.2 Oil from rape seed

For centuries, many plants have been used for the oil that they contain. Most supermarkets stock sunflower oil, corn oil and olive oil, as well as cooking oils that are mixtures of oils from several plants.

The food industry uses plant oils mainly for making margarine and in bakery products. Castrol, which lubricates the engines of high performance cars, gets its name because it contains oil from castor oil plants. London Transport tested a plant oil mixture in some of its vehicles and found it as good as the normal engine oils, refined from crude oil. Oil is also used in paint manufacture, and the treatment of wool and leather.

The first stage in extracting rape seed oil is to separate the seeds from dirt and stems. The next stage is to crack the tough skin of the seeds with rollers. Since rape seeds are quite small the machinery needs to be very carefully adjusted so that the seeds just crack. The cracked seeds are first cooked and then dried. After the seeds have been dried the water content goes down to about 3%. This dry mix goes to the pressers, which squeeze the oil out. The left-over waste goes to make animal feed.

Because the oil produced is still dirty, it must be cleaned and then refined. Cleaning involves leaving the oil in tanks to let the solids settle out and then filtering it to remove any final traces of solids. Refining involves dissolving the oil in a solvent which is then distilled to recover the pure oil. If it is going to be sold as cooking oil the final process is to bleach and de-odorize it.

After all that, manufacturers still call it 'pure, natural oil'!

A method of extracting oil used in India. Bullocks turn the heavy stone which grinds up the oil seeds.

Rape flowers are a brilliant yellow.

Global oil seed production 1980–1981 (million tonnes). The difference between oil + residue and total is waste.

Seed	Total	Oil content	Edible residue used as animal feed
Soya	87	16	69.6
Cotton seed	25	5	10.4
Groundnuts	12	5.5	6.0
Sunflower seed	15	5.7	9.0
Rape seed	11	4.3	6.5

1 Make a flow diagram to show the stages in the extraction of oil from rape seed.

2 You will need a calculator for this question. Make a table to show the percentage oil content of the crops shown in the table above, and the percentage waste.

3 Which one is the best source of oil? Suggest a reason why other oil crops are grown.

4 a) Use the table to suggest a more important use for soya. Soya comes out low as an oil producer.
b) Try to find other ways that we use soya.

2.3 Wonderful seaweeds

Seaweeds are surprisingly important plants although, often, we do not notice them at all. Seaweeds and phytoplankton are the producers for our coastal waters. Most of the fish we eat come from ecosystems that depend on these plants.

As well as being food for people and animals, seaweeds are useful for the substances which can be made from them (see Figure 1).

Making a jelly-like substance from some red seaweeds has a long history in the Far East. What they made was 'agar'. It is now mostly used for growing bacteria and fungi in science and hospital laboratories.

A large part of the seaweed industry is involved in extracting another jelly-like substance, **alginate**.

Figure 1.
A few of the traditional uses of seaweeds, which range from human food to sources of chemicals. The benefits from eating seaweed and from using it as a fertilizer probably both come from its relatively high trace element content.

Figure 2. Some examples of products that contain alginates.

Properties of alginates
A little alginate will absorb a lot of water, to make a very thick mixture. The 'gel' dries out very slowly. Alginates make a smooth mixture that can spread easily. If they are whipped into a foam they stay stable for a long time so the foam lasts. A more specialized property is that they are insoluble in hydrochloric acid, so they pass through the stomach undigested. This makes them useful for coating medicines that would be destroyed by the stomach's acid conditions before reaching the intestines where they are meant to be absorbed.

Trace elements in seaweed and grass. *Ascophyllum* is a type of seaweed. It can be ground up into a 'meal' for use as fertilizer or for adding to animal feed.

Element	*Ascophyllum* meal (g per tonne)	Grass (g per tonne)
Cobalt	1.5	0.14
Iodine	500	0.50
Copper	61	4.6
Boron	167	10
Iron	1132	56
Zinc	110	56

1 Make a 'spider' diagram to show as many uses of seaweed as you can.

2 Choose two products containing alginate from Figure 2. Explain how the properties of alginate are useful in them.

3 Seaweed is much harder to collect and extract minerals from than grass, and some minerals are more readily obtained from rocks. Use the information in the table to suggest the one mineral that would be worth extracting from seaweed. Explain your answer.

2.4 How does your garden grow?

Growing plants from seeds can be a tricky business. Whether they are planted indoors, in a greenhouse, or out of doors in a garden, they don't always come up. To find out what conditions are best for seeds to germinate or grow into seedlings, Clare and John set up the experiment described below.

They each soaked a packetful of sweet pea seeds in water. Clare then set up eight plant pots containing *sand*. She planted *ten* sweet pea seeds in each pot and then placed the pots in a variety of different places. She put two under a lamp in the room (20°C, in light) and two in a cupboard (20°C, in the dark). Two went in the fridge (5°C, in darkness) and the last pair in a specially lit part of the fridge (5°C, in light). She then carefully watered one of the pots in each place and left the other one dry.

John set up eight pots that were *exactly* similar to Clare's except they contained *clay* instead of sand.

All sixteen pots were left to see which would produce the most seedlings.

Some plants grow from bulbs. This lets them start their year's growth earlier than plants starting from seed.

Figure 1. The arrangement of the pots and the results after 10 days.

One factor that may affect how well seeds grow is the type of soil in which they are planted. Figure 2 shows in detail what the different soils look like under a microscope. Study them carefully and then answer in sentences the questions below.

1 Which soil has plenty of air but very little water?

2 Which soil has water but very little air?

3 Which soil has plenty of both air and water?

4 Which soil has very little air or water?

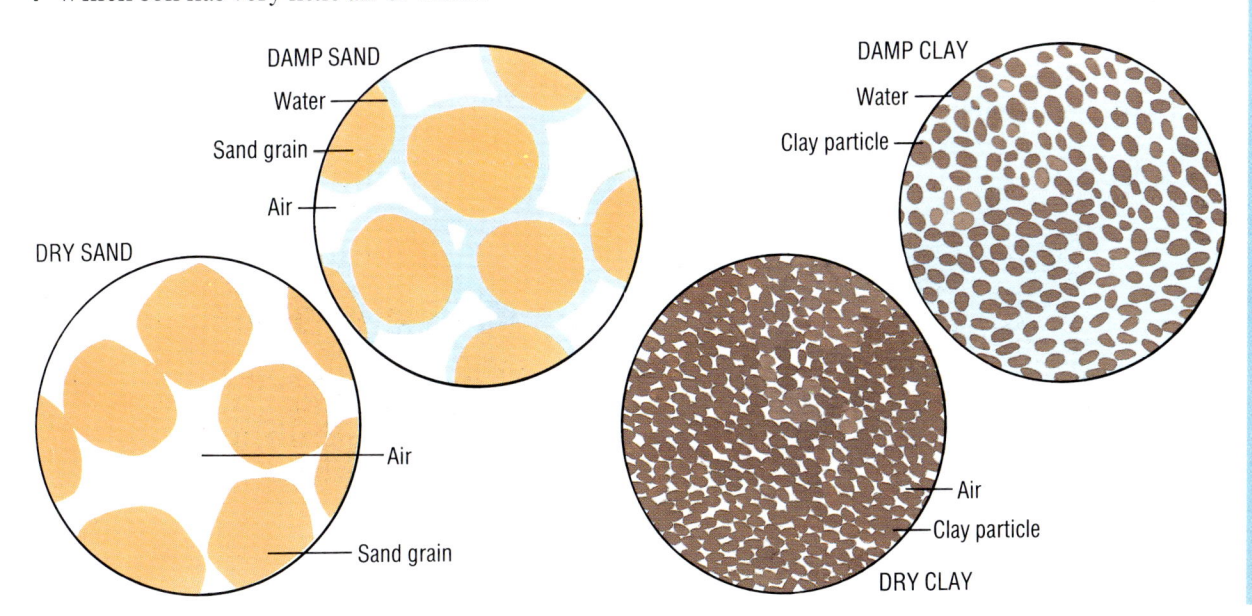

Figure 2. The appearance of different soils under the microscope.

To find out whether a particular condition helps seeds to grow or not, we need to compare the growth of the seeds in two pots which are different *only* in that particular condition. For example, to check on the effect of *light* we need to choose two pots that have the same soil and the same temperature but where one is in light and the other is in the dark. In this case we could compare pot A and pot E.

Look at the results shown in Figure 1.

5 Compare pot A with pot E. What do they tell us about the effect of light on how well sweet pea seeds grow?

6 Choose and write down the letters of a pair of pots we can compare to show the effect of watering the soil. What does the comparison show?

7 Now find and write down *another* pair of pots we could compare to check on the effects of watering. Does this pair show the same effect as your first pair, or not?

8 a) Which pots should we compare to find out whether sand or clay is better?

b) What condition does the sand/clay comparison show that the seeds need for growth?

9 a) Which two pots produced the most seedlings?
b) What conditions does this show to be important in helping seeds to grow?

10 According to the results, one condition seems to be more important than the others in helping seeds grow. Say which condition this is, and explain how you worked this out.

11 Seeds are usually planted underground. From the results of this experiment, suggest why this helps them to germinate. Explain your answer.

2.5 Light and shade

All green plants need light to carry out photosynthesis, but the amount of light available varies tremendously from place to place. Different plants have become adapted to different conditions of light and shade. So house plants, for example, are sold with labels which say where they will grow best.

Out-of-doors the variation in conditions is immense. For example, the tops of trees will be in the brightest light, while small plants growing on the ground among the trees will be shaded for most of the summer. One way of adapting to this shortage of light is to grow and flower early in the year, before the trees grow their new leaves. Many woodland plants, such as bluebell and celandine, have an early growing season. Another adaptation would be the ability to photosynthesize at low light intensities.

Indoor plants need different places.

The information and diagrams describe an experiment designed to compare how well three plants photosynthesize at different light levels. The experiment measured the rate of photosynthesis by checking the amount of carbon dioxide left around each type of leaf after it had been in the light for two hours. **Bicarbonate indicator** detects changes in the amount of carbon dioxide (CO_2) in samples of air. When the indicator is in contact with 'ordinary air' it is cherry red in colour. If the amount of CO_2 present increases, the indicator turns yellow. If the amount of CO_2 decreases, the indicator turns purplish.

These changes happen because CO_2 dissolves in water to form an acid, and the indicator changes colour with changes in acidity. Other acids or alkalis could also change the colour of the indicator, if they happened to make contact with it.

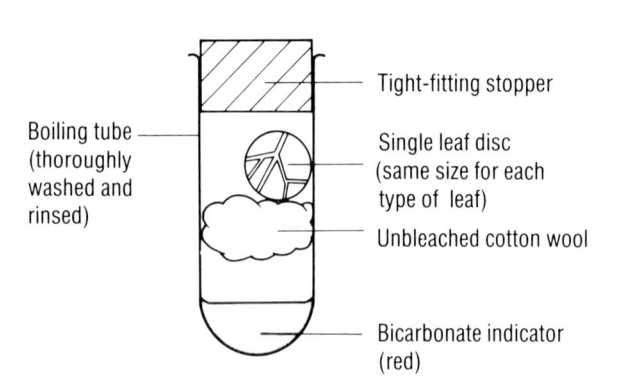

Figure 1. Experimental tube.

An investigation to compare the ability of plants to photosynthesize at different light intensities was carried out using bicarbonate indicator to show changes in production and use of CO_2. Some boiling tubes were set up as shown in Figure 1 and some were set up without leaf discs.

1 Describe clearly the various steps in setting up the boiling tube as shown in Figure 1.

2 What evidence is there in Figure 1 that the person who set it up knew that other acids and alkalis might change the indicator?

The leaf discs came from three different plants: Enchanter's nightshade, Bindweed and Privet.

Sets of four tubes were placed on a bench and illuminated by a powerful lamp – the arrangement is shown in plan view (from above) in Figure 2. Each set of four consisted of one tube for each type of leaf, plus one control tube with no leaf.

The light intensity (brightness) was measured using a light meter held just in front of each rack of tubes. The lamp was left on for 2 hours, then the colour of the indicator in each tube was noted. The results are shown in the table.

	Light intensity (lux)				
	2500	1500	1000	500	250
Enchanter's nightshade	Purple	Purple	Purple	Purple	Red
Bindweed	Purple	Purple	Purple	Red	Yellow
Privet	Red	Yellow	Yellow	Yellow	Yellow
Control	Red	Red	Red	Red	Red

Part of a student's note book.

Remember
PHOTOSYNTHESIS:
 Makes food
 Uses up carbon dioxide (CO_2)
RESPIRATION:
 'Burns' food
 Makes carbon dioxide (CO_2)

Figure 2. A plan view of the experiment.

Key:
B = bindweed
E = enchanter's nightshade
P = privet
O = no leaf disc (control)

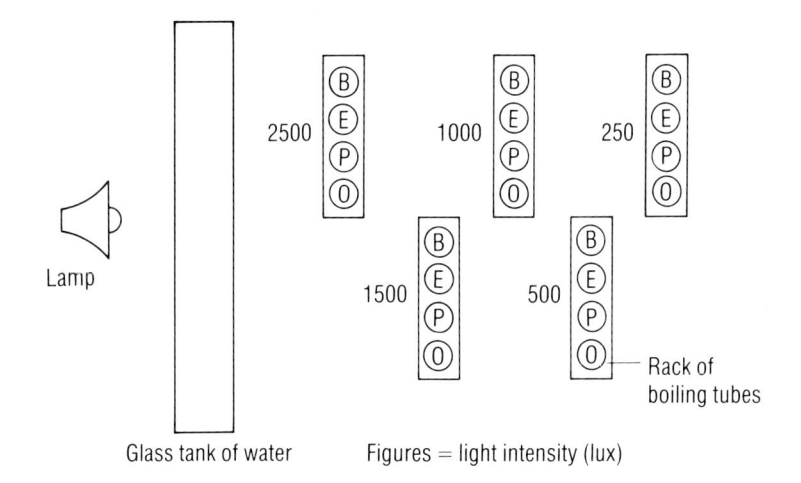

3 Suggest why a tank of water was put in front of the lamp.

4 Which colour in the results table shows that a leaf is photosynthesizing more than it is respiring?

5 For bindweed, explain how photosynthesis and respiration have produced the results in the five tubes.

6 Which of the three plants seems best adapted for growing in shady woodland and why?

2.6 A tale of two apples

'Don't throw your apple core in the fire, dear!' said Mrs Cox, 'I want to grow the pips!'

This was an historic moment. Had that apple core been thrown into the flames, you and I might never have tasted those crisp juicy apples known as Cox's Orange Pippins.

It was Christmas day in 1829 and the Cox family were settling down for a peaceful snooze after Christmas dinner when Mrs Cox made that fateful request. She laid the apple core with its nine pips on the mantlepiece to be attended to later.

Cox's Orange Pippins.

Bramley cooking apples.

'I'll tell you why,' she said.

'What, my dear?' her husband asked, trying to doze off in his arm chair.

'Why I want those seeds,' said Mrs Cox. 'That apple you had was a Ribston Pippin from the tree in the corner of the garden but in the summer I noticed that bees were carrying pollen to it from the other apple tree, you know, the Blenheim Orange by the hedge. The bees were coming mainly to one branch of the Ribston, so I tied a ribbon to that branch to remind me. I wanted to remember to grow the pips from apples from that branch, to see if the apples turn out to be unusual.'

True to her word Mrs Cox planted all nine seeds from the apple core. Only six germinated, and of these, four grew into rambling wild trees which gave only tiny sour apples, and one gave a tree with good cooking apples. The other pip, however, grew into a healthy strong tree with excellent eating apples. These came to be known as Cox's Orange Pippins, the result of cross-pollination between the Ribston Pippin and the Blenheim Orange.

These stories show us one very important thing about the seeds from any one plant. They vary quite considerably. In the natural environment plants produce seeds with a lot of **variation**. The result of this is that in a wide range of changing conditions some seedlings will always survive. Farmers and gardeners, however, want predictable results year after year and so avoid crops with a lot of variation. After choosing the best varieties farmers give them the best growing conditions to get the highest yield possible.

All the Cox's Orange Pippin trees in the world are derived from the one original tree in the story. To avoid the sort of variations found in seeds, **cuttings** were taken and grown up until they were big enough to produce their own crop. This process has been repeated over many years to provide more trees and therefore more apples.

Other new varieties have been discovered similarly. For example, in 1815 Mary Anne Brailsford grew a seedling which gave rise to all the modern Bramley cooking apples.

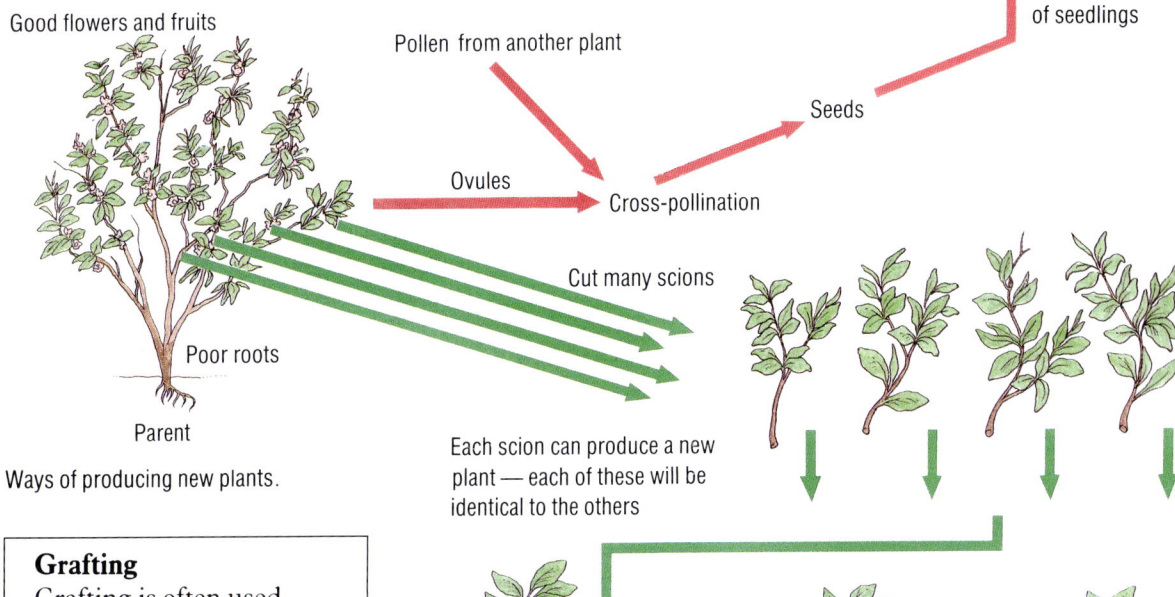

Ways of producing new plants.

Grafting

Grafting is often used with commercial plants such as rose bushes or fruit trees. A cutting called a scion from a good variety is fitted closely to the rootstock of a tougher variety. The tissues of the two grow together to produce a grafted plant. This has a good yield of high quality fruit or flowers on tough roots.

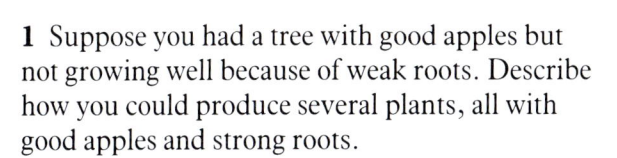

1 Suppose you had a tree with good apples but not growing well because of weak roots. Describe how you could produce several plants, all with good apples and strong roots.

2 If you were to plant seeds today from a Cox's Orange Pippin, would you expect to get identical plants from each pip? Explain your answer.

3 Why do grafts taken from a Cox's Orange Pippin or a Bramley always give predictable results?

4 Give as many reasons as you can for a commercial grower to produce more of a known variety by cuttings or grafts rather than seeds.

5 What main point is being made on these pages about the two possible ways of reproducing plants?

2.7 Mars Station One

There are plans to have permanent laboratories set up on the Moon and on Mars in the early years of next century. People will stay in them for months or even years to do long-term scientific research. The costs of sending food and oxygen all the way from Earth would be colossal, so the stations are planned to be completely self-sufficient for these essentials. They are to grow their own food and produce their own oxygen. 'Biosphere Two' is the first full scale trial of such a system.

The key to all this is, of course, photosynthesis by green plants.

Green plants take in carbon dioxide gas from the air, and water from the soil. They then use light energy from the sun to convert these raw materials into foods and oxygen. In poor growing conditions, when the plants can just survive, they need to make as much food and oxygen by photosynthesis as they use up in respiration. Under better growing conditions the plants produce more food and oxygen than they need. It is this extra that supplies the needs of animals – including humans. The plan is to arrange the conditions so that the plants do as much extra photosynthesis as possible.

The information below shows the results of experiments done to find the best conditions for the plants.

Biosphere II, a huge greenhouse in the middle of the Arizona Desert. It may one day provide a completely self-contained environment. Scientists will live there for two years, with all the food, air and water they need supplied by the ecosystem in the greenhouse. The only things they receive from the outside world will be radio and TV!

Oxygen production

Figure 1 shows how different light levels affect oxygen production by a plant growing in a greenhouse. The amount of oxygen produced shows how much photosynthesis is happening.

1 How much oxygen is produced when the light is at level 0?

2 What happens to the amount of oxygen produced when the light is increased to level 1 and then to level 2?

3 Between light level 0 and light level 2, what seems to control how much photosynthesis happens?

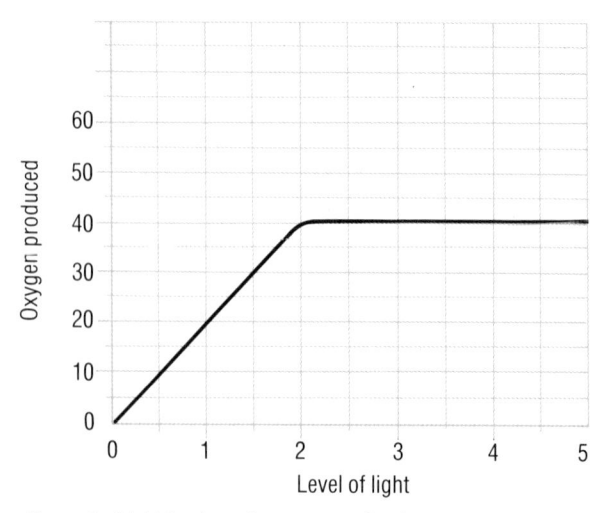

Figure 1. Light levels and oxygen production.

In a situation like this we often say that light is the limiting factor. If we give the plant more light, then it does more photosynthesis.

4 What happens to the amount of oxygen produced when the light is increased from level 2 to level 5?

Something seems to be preventing the plant from doing more photosynthesis – making more food and oxygen. We can see just what the problem is if we repeat the experiment using air with more carbon dioxide than normal. Figure 2 shows the results.

5 At light level 4, how much oxygen is produced when the air has 0.03% carbon dioxide?

6 What difference does it make if we increase the amount of carbon dioxide to 0.5% and then to 1.0%?

7 At light level 4, what seems to be limiting the amount of oxygen produced?

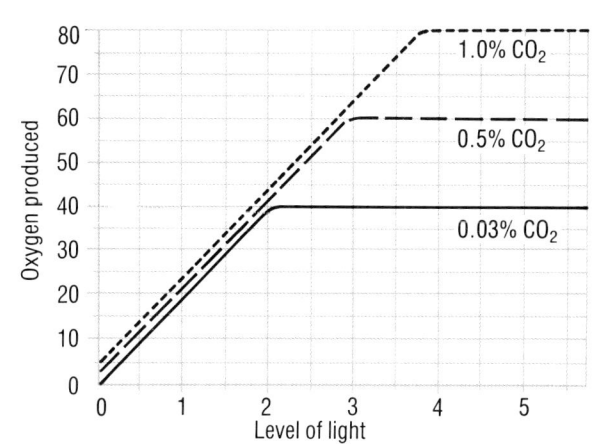

Figure 2. When the plant is given different levels of carbon dioxide.

Food production

The table shows the yield of tomato plants grown in air with different percentages of carbon dioxide in it. All the plants had the *same* amount of light.

8 Plot a graph to show the change in yield with different percentages of carbon dioxide.

9 What factor seems to be limiting growth at this light level?

10 The normal proportion of carbon dioxide on Earth is 300 p.p.m. How high would it be worth raising it, to maximize yield at this light level?

It is not only the supply of raw materials that controls how much photosynthesis happens. Figure 3 shows the effect of temperature on tomato growth.

11 What seems to be the optimum temperature for tomato growth?

12 What is the yield at this temperature?

13 People normally live in air with very little (0.03%) carbon dioxide in it, and are comfortable at around 20 °C. Explain why the designers of Biosphere Two split the building into several separate compartments.

Yield of tomatoes at different CO_2 levels

Carbon dioxide (parts per million)	Tomato yield (kg/m^2)
50	2.0
150	3.7
250	5.0
430	6.6
600	7.5
790	8.1
1000	8.2
1200	8.2

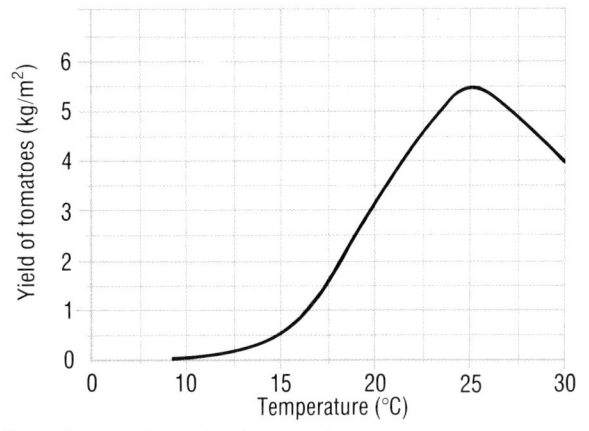

Figure 3. Tomato yield and temperature.

3.1 Building bodies

The food we eat supplies the building materials and the energy our body needs. But how can muscle and bone be built from bread, meat and milk? To understand this we need to know how the foods themselves are built up.

We are what we eat, but not quite like this!

Everything in the world (including food and bodies) is made up of very tiny building blocks called atoms. **Atoms** are so tiny that there are over a million atoms in the full stop at the end of this sentence.

Elements are the simplest kind of substances, made of only one kind of atom. Carbon, hydrogen and oxygen are common elements in living things. Nitrogen, iron and phosphorus are some of the others. There are 92 naturally occurring elements.

Most substances are made from two or more different kinds of atom. These substances are called **compounds**.

Atoms are almost always stuck together in groups. Each group is called a **molecule**.

Each element, like oxygen or carbon, has only *one* kind of atom in its molecules. The molecules of a compound have *several* kinds of atoms in them.

Chemical changes happen when atoms and molecules rearrange to form different groups. New compounds are made, often with very different properties!

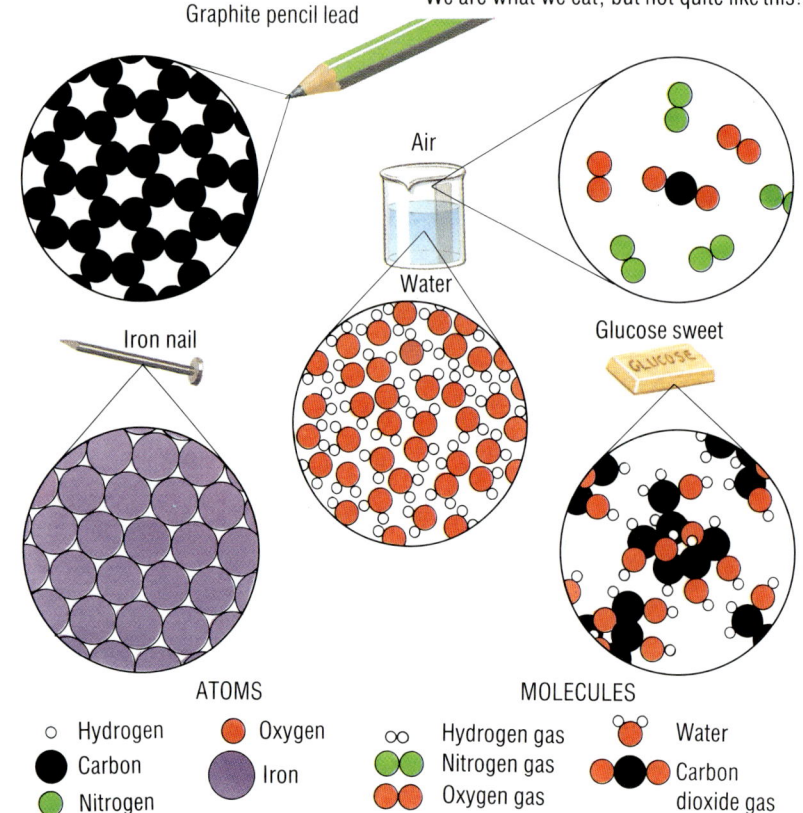

ATOMS
- ○ Hydrogen
- ● Carbon
- ● Nitrogen
- ● Oxygen
- ● Iron

MOLECULES
- ∞ Hydrogen gas
- Nitrogen gas
- Oxygen gas
- Water
- Carbon dioxide gas

Figure 1. Atoms and molecules.

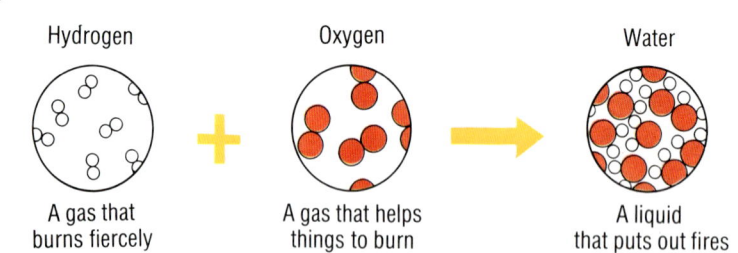

Hydrogen — A gas that burns fiercely + Oxygen — A gas that helps things to burn → Water — A liquid that puts out fires

Figure 2. A chemical change.

Look at Figure 1, and then answer these questions in sentences.

1 a) Which kinds of atoms are in the graphite pencil 'lead'?

b) Is graphite an element or a compound?

2 a) Which atoms are in the molecules of water?

b) Is water an element or a compound?

3 Which material is shown to be a mixture of different kinds of molecules? Write down what the molecules are and whether they are elements or compounds.

4 Draw a table to show which of the materials shown in Figure 1 are *elements* and which are *compounds*.

Most of the nutrients in our food are compounds made of large molecules. These large molecules are made by smaller molecules linking together. It is simplest to show the large molecules as **block diagrams**. These do not show all the atoms, but just the small molecules which build up the large ones.

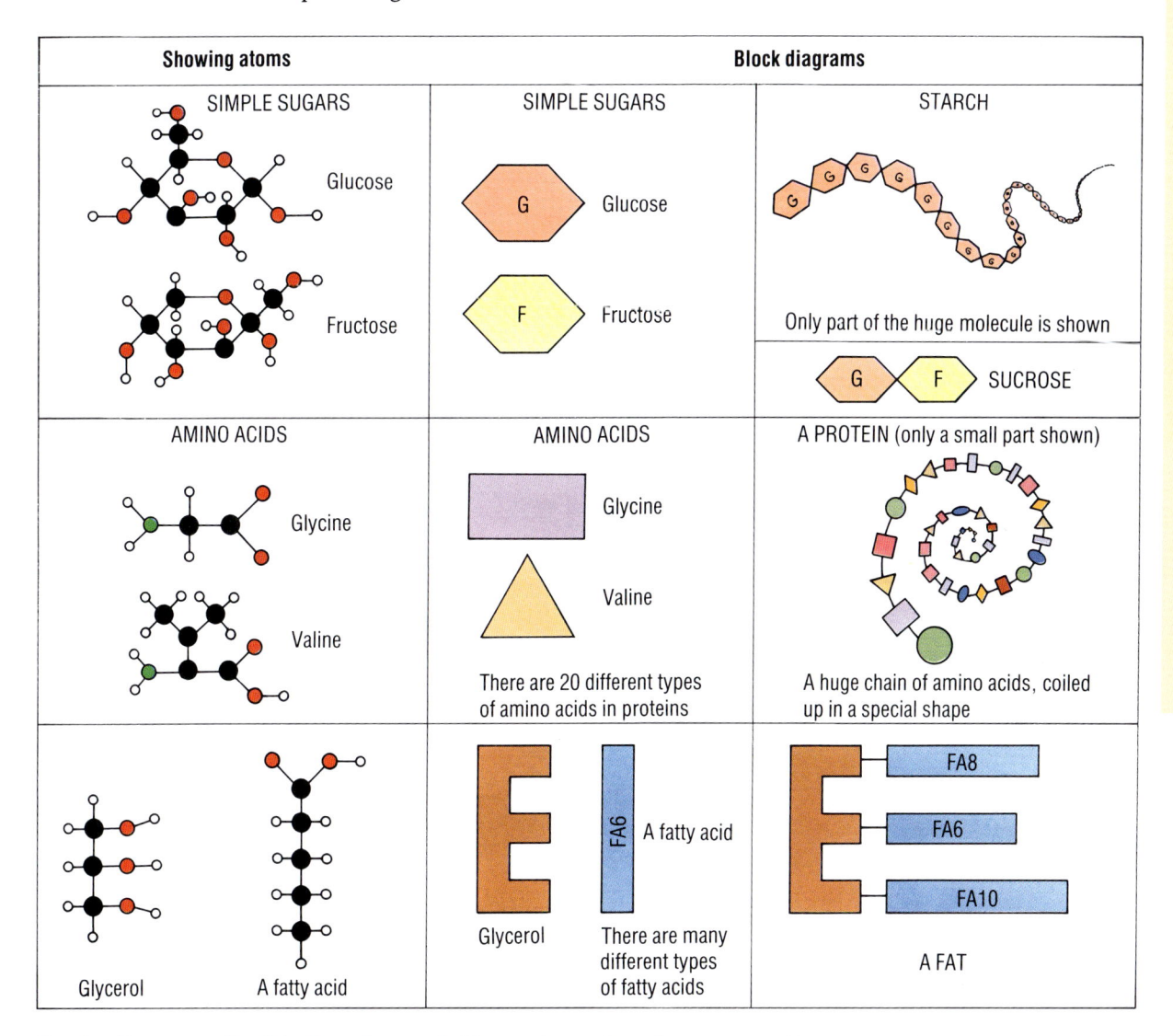

Figure 3. How food molecules are built up.

Our bodies can only absorb and use *soluble* nutrients, but these large molecules do *not* dissolve. They must be broken down into the small molecules of which they are made. This is what happens when food is digested.

5 What small molecules join to make up:
a) a sucrose molecule?
b) a fat molecule?

6 What will be produced when these nutrients are fully digested?
a) starch
b) protein.

7 What chemical element is in amino acids and proteins but not in sugars, starch or fats?

8 Maltose is a 'double sugar' like sucrose and is made by the part-digestion of starch. Draw and label a block diagram of a molecule of maltose.

9 Starch molecules are all very alike. Explain why protein molecules can be so different.

10 In aerobic respiration, carbon dioxide gas is produced. What atoms does it contain and where have they come from?

3.2 Chance would be a fine thing

Most species of animal have some form of sexual reproduction. For this they produce special sex cells, the eggs and sperms. When a sperm meets and fuses with an egg at fertilization, a new individual begins. But how can eggs and sperms be brought together? After all, the animals producing them may be living in different places, or they may be aggressive towards others of the same species.

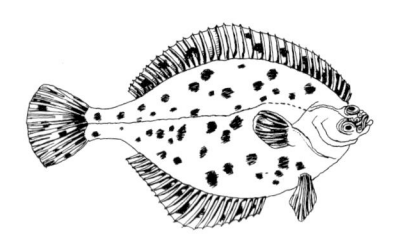

Since gametes can survive in water for a time, aquatic animals can simply release their eggs and sperms into the water, and leave the rest to chance. This may be simple, but it is wasteful. To make sure that at least some eggs are fertilized they have to release *very large numbers* of eggs and sperms. Making all these eggs and sperms uses up a great deal of food. If most of them never meet, then it is wasted.

The table opposite shows some information about reproduction in various species of fish. Some of these fish have special features (or **adaptations**) that make fertilization less a matter of chance. Some behave in special ways to make fertilization more likely. An example of behaviour which reduces the wastage of eggs and sperms is the way the fish gather together in shoals at spawning time.

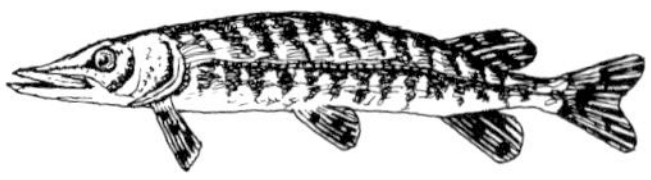

The small table below shows some adaptations of fish that increase the chances of fertilization.

1 Draw a table like the one below and put each fish in the column of the adaptation it shows. (Some will go in two columns.)

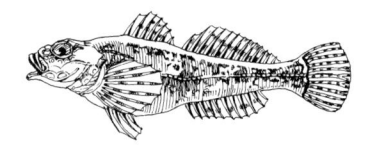

Where and when fish release eggs and sperm, to help bring them together.

Similar place	Similar time	Same special place	Exactly the same place	Sperms inside female

Plaice, about 50 cm long

Dogfish, about 65 cm long

'Mermaid's purse' (egg case)

Pike, about 130 cm long

Miller's thumb, about 12 cm long

2 If we assume that *fewer* eggs are needed when fertilization is *more* certain, then
a) which of the above adaptations is most effective and why?
b) which method is least effective?

3 Plaice and roach are roughly the same size, and have similar breeding behaviour, but one is marine and the other lives in fresh water. Find another pair of species, roughly the same size, one from each habitat. What evidence is there from these four species that marine fish tend to produce more eggs than fresh water fish?

4 Miller's Thumb and Minnow are roughly the same size, and both live in the same habitat. Find another pair of species which have the same size and habitat. Look at the numbers of eggs produced by all four fish.
a) What evidence is there that the larger the number of eggs produced the smaller each egg is?
b) What evidence is there that the more certain fertilization is, the fewer eggs are laid?

5 What evidence is there that, after fertilization, the parents protect small eggs less than medium sized eggs? Suggest reasons why.

Reproductive strategies of some fishes

Species	Habitat	Average length (cm)	Approximate no. of eggs per female	Diameter of egg (mm)	Fertilization
Brown trout	river / lake	25–40	1000	5.0	Female makes hollow in gravel. Male and female lie side by side in hollow, releasing eggs and sperm at the same time. Female covers eggs with gravel.
Cod	sea	80–100	500 000–5 000 000	1.5	Eggs and sperm released in to surrounding sea water as fish swim together in large groups in spring. Fertilized eggs float in plankton.
Grayling	river	25–50	3000–6000	3.0	Female makes a pit in gravel. Eggs and sperm are released in the pit at the same time. Female covers eggs with gravel.
Lesser spotted dogfish	sea	60–100	18–20	60.0 (not to scale)	Male courts female and mates with her, passing sperm into the female's body. Fertilization occurs before the eggs are laid.
Ling	sea	100–150	20 000 000–60 000 000	1.0	Eggs and sperm released into the sea when the fish swim together in groups in spring. Fertilized eggs float in the plankton.
Miller's thumb	river	10–15	100–200	2.5	Male digs a pit under a large stone, courts female, which lays eggs in the pit. Male later sheds sperm over the eggs. He guards eggs until they hatch.
Minnow	river / lake	7–10	200–1000	1.0	Males and females swim together in groups releasing eggs and sperm into the water in spring. Fertilized eggs fall and stick to stones.
Pike	river / lake	100–150	40 000–400 000	2.5	Eggs and sperm released into the water as males and females swim together. Fertilized eggs stick to plants.
Plaice	sea	25–40	50 000–1 000 000	1.5	Males and females gather in the same area. Eggs and sperm released into the sea water in mid-winter. Fertilized eggs float in plankton.
Roach	river / lake	25–30	50 000–100 000	1.0	Males and females swim among vegetation, releasing eggs and sperm into the water at the same time.

KEY: ≈ sea. ≋ river. ⁙ lake.
Eggs are actual size, except dogfish

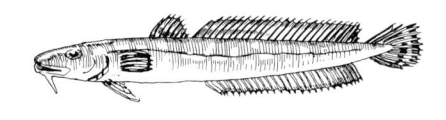

Ling, about 125 cm long

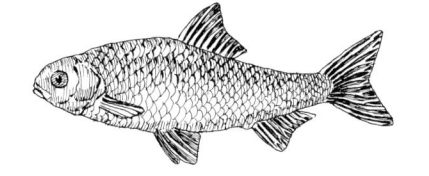

Roach, about 28 cm long

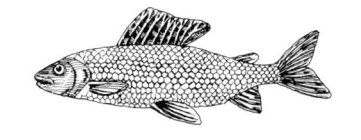

Grayling, about 35 cm long

3.3 Voyage of the Gutbug

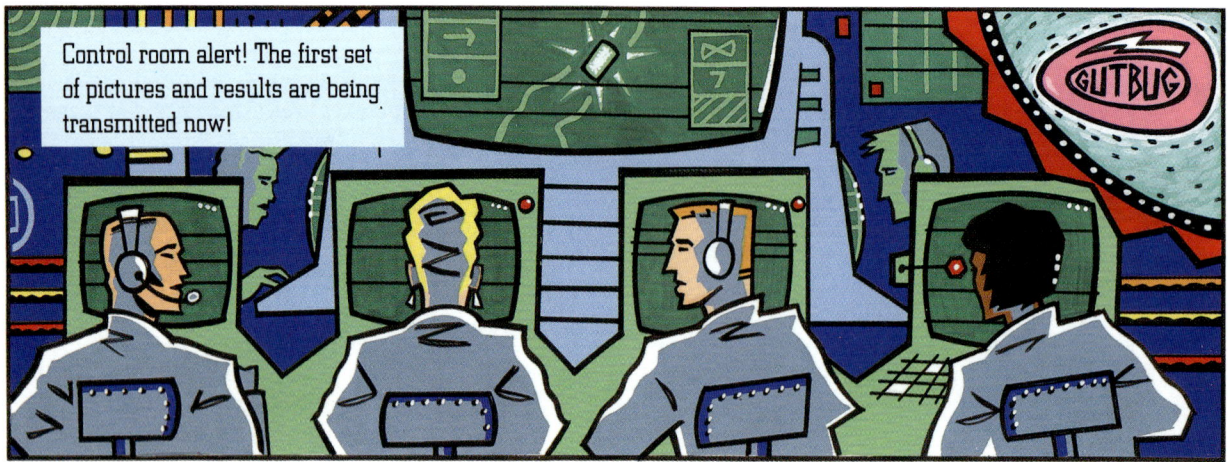

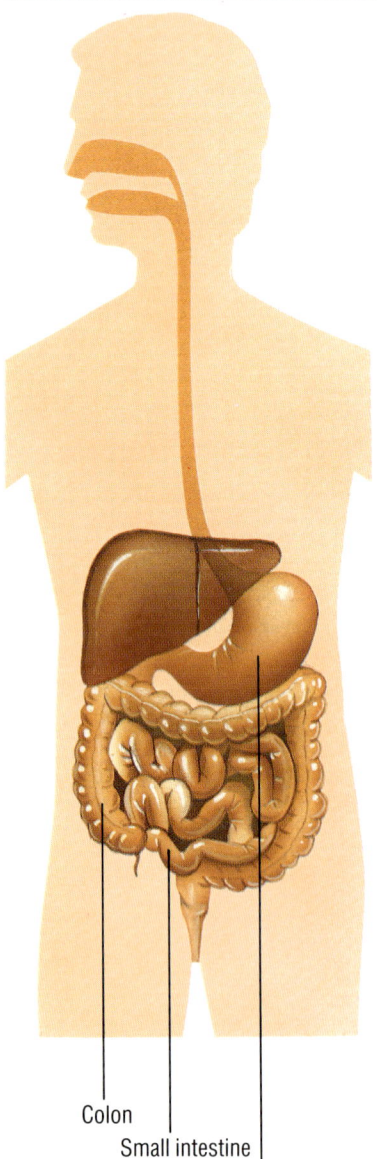

Control room alert! The first set of pictures and results are being transmitted now!

The research teams were trying out a new approach to studying the digestive system. A patient had volunteered to swallow a very sophisticated new piece of apparatus about the size of a Brazil nut. It was nicknamed the 'Gutbug'.

It would pass through the patient's digestive system, carrying out tests and transmitting information back to the control room computers. A voice synthesizer allowed Gutbug to make instant progress reports and pictures were relayed to six video monitor screens. Gutbug was also equipped with a set of miniature jaws which could take a biopsy. A small piece of tissue could be nipped off and returned for analysis.

Gutbug to control! Have been forced down the oesophagus by the muscular contractions of peristalsis, and am now in the stomach. Have carried out a pH squirt test with indicator and found conditions acid as expected. Large lumps of food being broken down. I'm being tossed around as the muscles of the stomach walls squeeze the food backwards and forwards. Enzyme probe detects presence of pepsin which is breaking down proteins.

The control room staff watched their instruments and waited for the next transmission. The wrinkled muscular sides of the stomach could be seen, churning up the food.

Gutbug to control! Entering duodenum! Sensors picking up high levels of bile and pancreatic enzymes. Squirt test detects change in pH showing alkaline conditions. Enzymes present include trypsin, breaking down proteins to amino acids, amylase turning starch to maltose, and lipase breaking down fats to fatty acids and glycerol.

As I move into ileum, digestion of foods continuing and absorption of nutrients into the bloodstream proceeding as normal.

Colon
Small intestine
Stomach

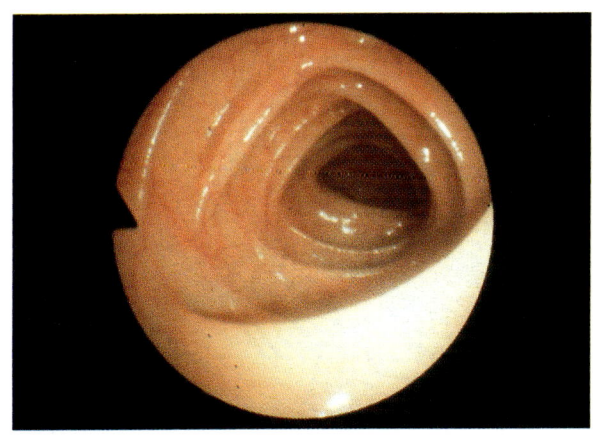

Levels of amino acids and glucose going down as they are absorbed by villi of the intestine wall. Glycerol and fatty acids passing into lymph vessels. Will report back to control in two hours.

Tension started to mount in the control room.

The next part of the journey was the most important. Gutbug was about to perform a 'grab test', by using tiny retractable jaws to pinch off a tiny piece of colon tissue, and bring it back for examination in the laboratory.

Gutbug to control! Entering large intestine! A lot of movement here! Being blasted along by pockets of gas! Absorption of water and minerals into the bloodstream seem to be far from normal, leading to watery conditions, and evidence of bleeding from the walls of the bowel. Switching to close-image focusing to show damage.

Counting down to grab test in ten seconds! . . . Three! Two! One!   Grab!

The miniature jaws did their work. The sample would be studied later in the lab.

Gutbug to control! Mission completed! Looking forward to coming out of here!

The inside of the small intestine, as seen with an endoscope.

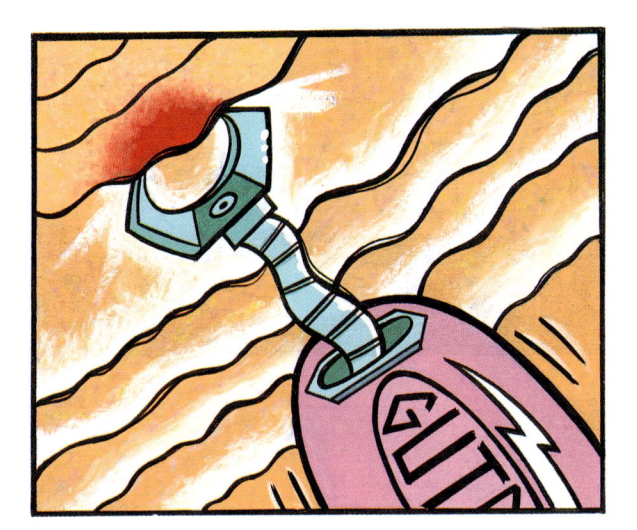

Gutbug 'grab-test'.

1 How was the Gutbug propelled through the digestive system?

2 Name two chemicals detected in the stomach.

3 In what two ways was food being broken down here?

4 What reports did the Gutbug make about pH conditions?

5 The Gutbug sent back pictures of finger-like structures, in the small intestine. What are these called, and what is their function?

6 Where did the Gutbug first detect the presence of bile? Where does bile come from, and what does it do to food in the gut?

7 Copy and complete the table below based on information transmitted by the Gutbug.

8 In the small intestine, why did the Gutbug detect a fall in levels of nutrients such as amino acids and glucose?

9 What was wrong with the patient, and in what ways was the Gutbug able to investigate this?

Position	Food being digested	Enzyme	Products from digested foods
Duodenum	Protein	?	? acids
	?	Amylase	Maltose
	Fat	?	Fatty acids and ?

3.4 Producing convincing evidence

We talk about food and drink as separate items in our diet but nearly all food has water in it. Oranges and tomatoes are obviously very watery, but even biscuits and dry corn flakes have *some* water in them.

The usual way of estimating the water in a food involves weighing the food, drying it to remove the water, and then weighing the food again. Exactly how you do this affects how accurate a result you get.

The results below were obtained by four different teams of investigators.

Each team started with one 10 g sample of each food. They dried the foods by the methods described below, and weighed them again. From the weight of the dried food they worked out the weight of water in each 10 g sample of food. The table shows their results.

Weight of water (g) in each 10 g sample of food

Team	Meat	Cucumber	Egg	Rice (uncooked)
A	5.4	8.2	6.3	0.9
B	5.9	8.7	6.8	1.0
C	6.9	9.4	7.8	1.1
D	6.5	9.8	7.2	1.3

Team A
This team put each 10 g sample in a dish. They put lids on the dishes to stop food falling out. They then decided that they had to stick the lids down so that mice in the lab could not knock the lids off and eat bits of their samples at night. Then they put the dishes on a shelf above a radiator. It was at 25 °C in the day time but only 15 °C at night. After 24 hours they reweighed their samples.

Team C
They put each 10 g sample, roughly chopped, in a dish and then put it in an oven set at 100 °C for 24 hours. They weighed the samples and then put them back into the oven for another 24 hours before weighing the samples again. If there was no change in weight they used that figure for their calculations. If the food has lost weight they put it back in the oven for another 24 hours and repeated the process until it lost no more weight between two weighings.

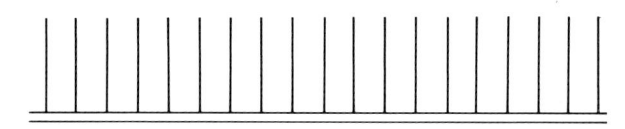

Gerbils can survive for months without drinking water.

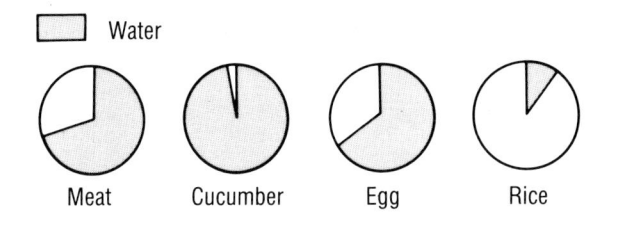

Water

Meat Cucumber Egg Rice

Team B
This team carefully chopped each sample into tiny even-sized pieces. They reweighed each sample after chopping to make sure that they had not lost any. Then they decided that they were losing juice on the chopping board so they started again chopping the food on weighed filter paper. At last they put each 10 g sample in a dish and then left it in an oven set at 100 °C for one hour. At the end of the hour they reweighed the samples.

Team D
They used exactly the same method as team C.

1 Which method should give the most accurate results and why?

2 What are two possible causes of inaccuracies in team A's method?

3 What is a possible cause of inaccuracy in team B's method?

4 Why do teams C and D *not* get the same answers?

5 a) Given all these results decide how to calculate the best figure of the water content of these four foods.
b) Explain why you have chosen this method.

6 a) Using the method you gave for Question 5, calculate the weight of water in each type of food. Put your results in a table, with an extra space for percentage of water.
b) Calculate the percentage of water in each food and enter it in your table.

7 Draw bar charts to show the percentage of water in each of these four foods.

8 Some days later, a fifth team did the same experiment, using team C's method. Their results are shown in the four pie charts.
a) In what ways are their results different from those of team C?
b) Suggest possible reasons for the differences.

3.5 Replacing the kidneys

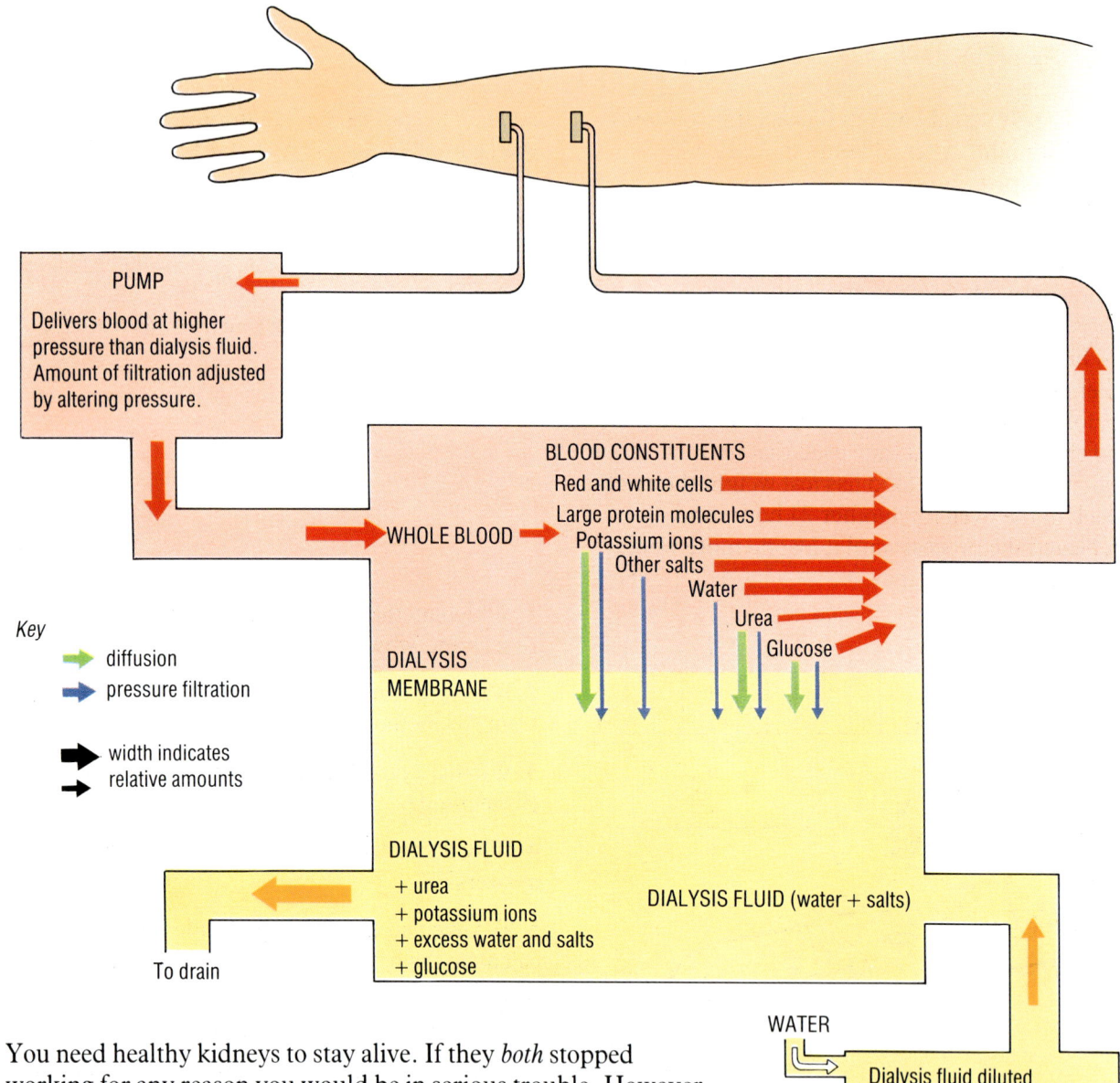

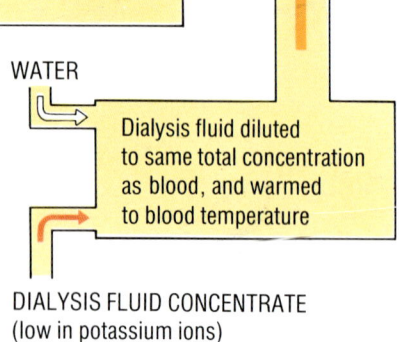

Key
→ diffusion
→ pressure filtration

→ width indicates
→ relative amounts

PUMP
Delivers blood at higher pressure than dialysis fluid. Amount of filtration adjusted by altering pressure.

WHOLE BLOOD

BLOOD CONSTITUENTS
Red and white cells
Large protein molecules
Potassium ions
Other salts
Water
Urea
Glucose

DIALYSIS MEMBRANE

DIALYSIS FLUID (water + salts)

DIALYSIS FLUID
+ urea
+ potassium ions
+ excess water and salts
+ glucose

To drain

WATER

Dialysis fluid diluted to same total concentration as blood, and warmed to blood temperature

DIALYSIS FLUID CONCENTRATE
(low in potassium ions)

Figure 1. Simplified flow diagram of a kidney machine.

You need healthy kidneys to stay alive. If they *both* stopped working for any reason you would be in serious trouble. However, you can lead a normal life with only one kidney. You can even survive with as little as 10% of your kidney tissues working. But with less than about 5% working you would probably die within two weeks.

If your kidneys had failed completely, you could control your salt and water balance by regulating what you eat and drink but you could not remove urea from your blood. Your survival would then depend on replacing the useless kidneys before the urea level rose high enough to kill you. If a suitable kidney from someone else was available you could have a transplant. If no transplant was possible your only alternative would be to have dialysis for several hours every few days. This is done using an 'artificial kidney', or **kidney machine**.

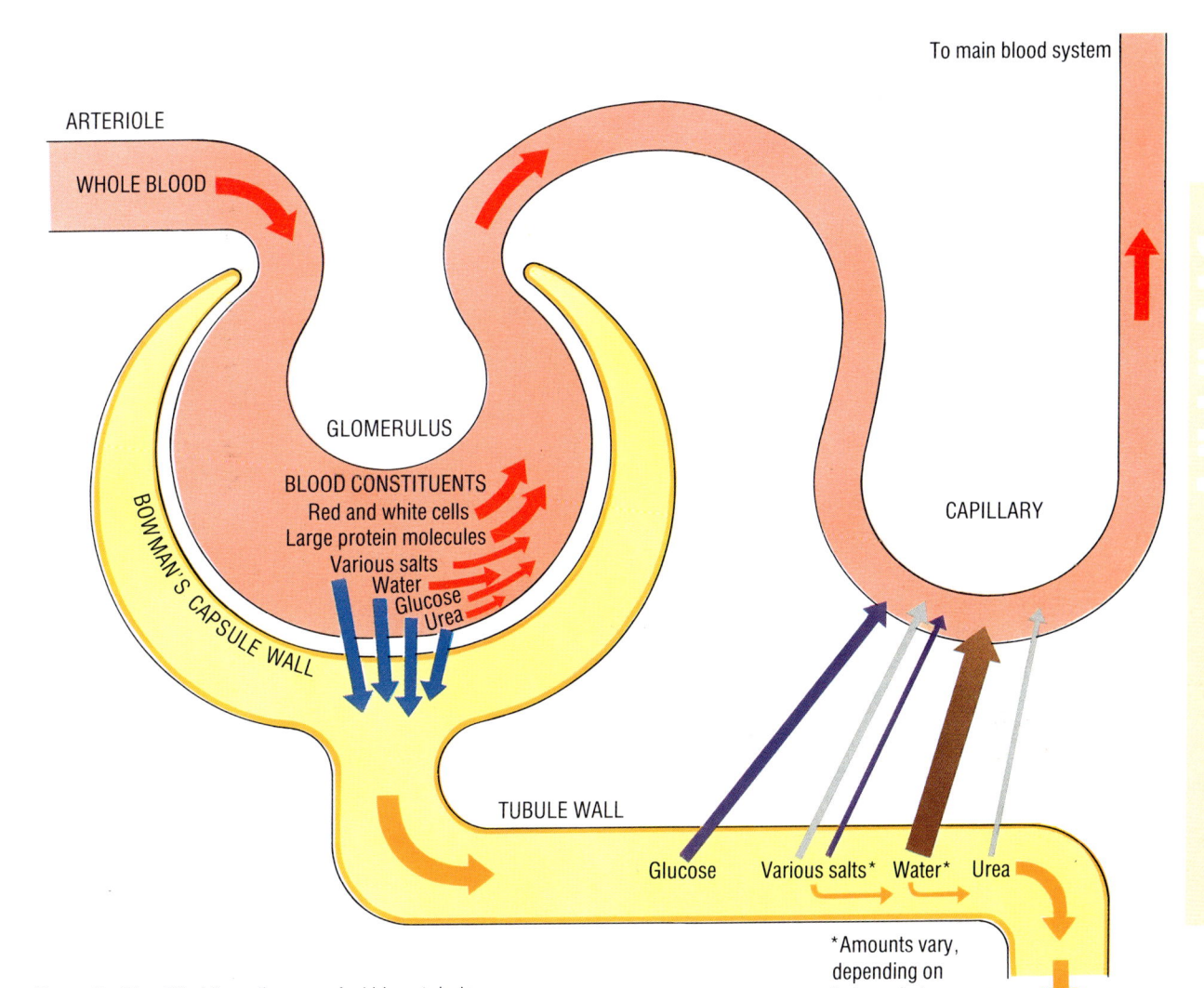

Figure 2. Simplified flow diagram of a kidney tubule.

*Amounts vary, depending on balance between intake and amount needed.

URINE (water + urea + salts) to bladder

Key
→ pressure filtration   → diffusion
→ active transport   → osmosis
➡ width indicates relative amounts

Kidney machines contain a special, artificial membrane called a dialysis membrane (rather like Visking tubing). It acts as a very fine filter, in the same sort of way as the wall of a Bowman's capsule in a real kidney. Figure 1 is a simple flow diagram showing how a kidney machine works. Of course, the real thing is much more complicated, with a large surface area of membrane arranged in many layers. Figure 2 shows a similar diagram of a kidney tubule, for comparison.

1 Write a description of how the artificial kidney works. You should mention:
a) where the blood is taken from and pumped to.
b) which materials cannot cross the membrane, and why.
c) which materials do cross the membrane and why.
d) what controls the rate of filtration.

2 If dialysis fluid was supplied at a concentration more dilute than blood, what would be the effects on the patient's blood?

3 An excess of potassium ions in the blood is dangerous, as too much leads to heart failure. How does the artificial kidney prevent an excess of potassium ions?

4 a) If a normal person drank an excessive amount of water, how would the kidney tubule deal with it?
b) If someone on dialysis drank an excessive amount of water, how could the kidney machine be adjusted to remove more from the blood?

5 Which two processes are shown to occur in living kidneys but not in the artificial kidney?

3.6 Water, water everywhere

In each of the pictures on these two pages, the amount of water in a person's body is changing. Too much or too little water can damage cells, or stop them working. The amount of water in the body has to remain fairly constant, so any change in the amount entering or leaving the body is followed by something happening to restore water balance. For example, if you drink a lot of water, you produce a lot of urine soon afterwards.

The table shows water intake and output by an average-sized person in different situations for one day. The first column shows normal figures for someone spending most of the day indoors in comfortable temperatures. As you can see, in columns 1 and 2 the total amount of water going into the body is balanced by the same amount leaving the body.

The sweat this girl is losing is mostly water.

Water balance in various conditions (figures are cm^3/day)

		1 Normal day	2 Day outside in cold weather	3 Day with 5-hour disco	4 Day of fun run	5 Diarrhoea attack	6 Day in hot desert
WATER IN	In drinks	1500	1500	3500		3000	500
	In food	800	800	800	1000	200	400
	From burning of food	300	300	300	500	300	300
	Total	2600	2600	4600		3500	1200
WATER OUT	Urine	1100	1500		1200	600	500
	Sweat	1000	600	1500	3000	1000	4000
	Evaporation from lungs	400	400	500	600	400	600
	In faeces	100	100	100	100		100
	Total	2600	2600		4900		5200

1 Copy the table and fill in the blanks in columns 3, 4 and 5 by working out the volumes needed to achieve balance.

In column 2 there are two differences from 'normal'. The amount of urine produced is greater, and the amount of sweat is less. This could be explained by saying that on a cold day a person sweats less. With less water lost by sweating more must be removed in some other way. Extra urine is produced, so reducing the body's amount of water to normal.

2 Suggest explanations for each of the differences from normal in columns 3, 4 and 5.

3 Assume that on a 'normal' day, this person urinates (passes urine) five times. How many times would you expect him or her to urinate on a cold day?

Not much sweat is lost on a day like this!

Delicious to eat, but it's mostly water!

When there is no balance

People will die if water loss reaches 20% of body weight.

Sometimes it is not possible to achieve a balance between intake and output – for example, if someone is stranded in the desert. Column 6 of the table shows a situation like this.

4 What is the net loss of water per day from this person?

5 If the person in column 6 weighs 60 kg to begin with, how many days will he survive? (1000 cm^3 of water weighs 1 kg.)

6 Diarrhoea can cause death by dehydration very quickly in babies. Suppose that a 5 kg baby normally drinks 1000 cm^3 of milk per day. Assume that its normal output of fluid will be 1000 cm^3. (Output and input won't quite balance, since the baby is growing.) Suppose that this baby develops diarrhoea, losing 1200 cm^3 of her fluid per day, and is so weak that she can only drink 700 cm^3. How long would you expect her to survive?

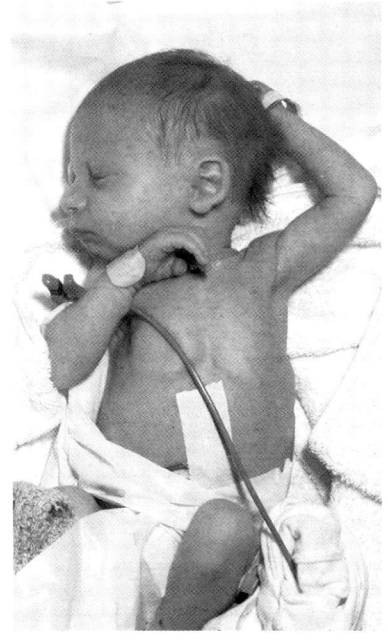

Water loss may kill this child.

3.7 Moonbugs

On a remote asteroid, advance parties testing mineral deposits noticed a grey film on some of the rocks. Running over this film were tiny tracks, leading to small channels penetrating deep into the rock. Samples of the rock were returned to base, and the film was found to be made of bacteria. But what made the tracks?

Video cameras and environment sensors were set up and left to monitor the scene. Pictures were beamed to the base and were now being studied by space biologists. The cameras slowly scanned the scene. Readings of temperature, light and humidity were shown in a corner of the screen.

In the first beams of sunrise, small armour-plated creatures came in their thousands from the channels in the rock, where they had been sheltering from the intense cold of the long night. Some had legs or antennae or plates missing, perhaps the result of previous battles in the struggle for survival.

A moonbug.

'Well, here they come!' said Chris. 'We're the first humans to see this sight!'

'Do you notice anything about their distribution?' asked Alex. 'They're not evenly spread, are they? They seem to bunch together.'

'Yes, they're homing in on the pockets of bacteria. This must be their only food supply.'

The temperature was 8°C, and the humidity was high. The light was dim, almost completely dark. The creatures wandered about slowly, grazing on the bacteria.

Gradually, the sun came up with searing heat over the harsh rugged landscape. Quite suddenly the small armour-plated creatures started to scramble for their subterranean labyrinth. One or two individuals were overturned in the rush and tiny babies could be seen, pale and delicate, clinging on underneath.

Underground, conditions would be cooler and more humid, more like conditions on the surface when they had emerged to feed. But those conditions were now quickly changing, with temperatures of 60°C, bright light and rapidly dropping humidity.

When the last few creatures were scampering into their burrows, the light was blinding, the temperature had risen to 130°C and humidity was almost zero. Soon, no creatures were to be seen except for a few badly mutilated individuals trampled in the rush. They curled up and turned black as the temperature reached 200°C.

The moonbugs' environment.

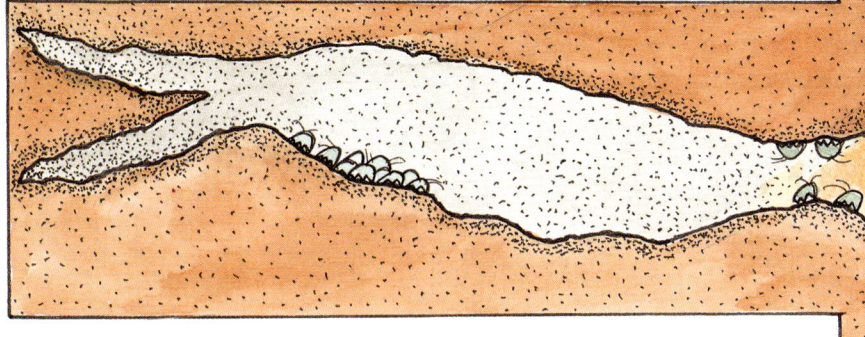

'Well, that was pretty dramatic when the sun came up. They didn't like that one little bit!' said Chris.

'No, that's true,' replied Alex. 'My guess is we won't see any more action till the sun goes down again in six hours. Let's check out till then.'

When they got back a few individuals were emerging. The short scorching day was over and the long dark night approached. The creatures collected in groups in the shadows of the rocks, where conditions were sheltered and the first condensation of precious moisture would occur in the cooler 'evening' of their day.

1 What extreme conditions were the creatures avoiding during:
a) the asteroid 'day'?
b) the asteroid 'night'?

2 Which three conditions in the environment would the sun change as it rose to its full height?

3 What kinds of protection would the babies get by being carried underneath the parents?

4 Suppose that some of the creatures were brought back to Earth. Describe experiments you could do to find out which of the three conditions in Question 2 the creatures responded to fastest.
a) Decide how you could investigate one condition at a time.
b) Draw diagrams to show what equipment you would use and say what you would do.
c) State how you could tell which condition made them react quickest.

5 Pick one of the times described in the story. Draw the video screen, showing the picture seen by the camera and the data recorded by the sensors.

ANIMALS

49

4.1 Diffusion

The molecules of all substances are constantly moving. Molecules of gases, liquids and of substances in solution move away from a place where there is a lot of the material to a place where there is less. This spreading out is called **diffusion**.

In diffusion, molecules can only move between places where there is a concentration difference, always moving *from* the higher *to* the lower concentration. If there is no concentration difference there is no diffusion.

In living organisms the diffusion of substances dissolved in water is very important. Diffusion can occur between cells and their surroundings. 'Surroundings' may be 'outside' as in Figure 1, or liquids inside the body, like plasma for a blood cell. Substances also diffuse in the cytoplasm of the cell. Sometimes substances diffuse right through thin layers of cells. Examples of this are found in gas exchange organs such as lungs, plant leaves and fish gills.

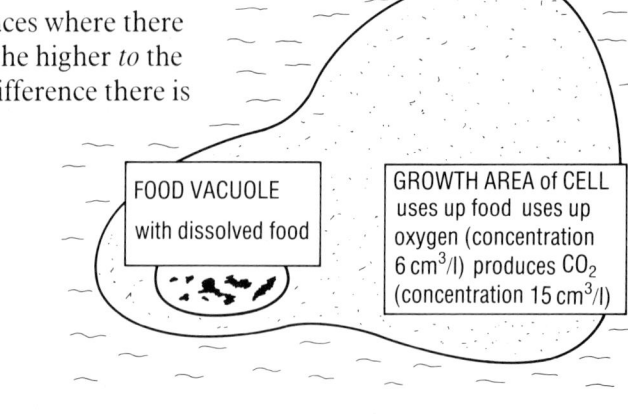

POND WATER
Oxygen concentration 7 cm^3/l
CO_2 concentration 8 cm^3/l

FOOD VACUOLE with dissolved food

GROWTH AREA of CELL uses up food uses up oxygen (concentration 6 cm^3/l) produces CO_2 (concentration 15 cm^3/l)

Figure 1. A single-celled pond animal.

Baby in womb

Mother's blood and baby's blood next to each other in the placenta

Key
← Movement of blood
⇐ Diffusion of sugars and other foods
⇐ Diffusion of wastes

Comparison of gases in mother's and baby's blood

	Mother's artery to placenta	Baby's artery to placenta
Units of oxygen	95	45
Units of carbon dioxide	46	60.4

Figure 2. Notice where the placenta is.

1 a) Copy Figure 1.
b) Draw arrows on your diagram to show which way each of the three substances is moving.
c) Describe the diffusion of food substances that would occur inside the cell.
d) Describe the diffusion that would occur between this single-celled animal and its surroundings.

2 a) Copy Figure 3.
b) Use the table to decide which way the oxygen and carbon dioxide move across the cells that separate the mother's blood from the baby's blood.
c) Add arrows (in different colours) to your diagram showing the movement of oxygen and of carbon dioxide. (Add these arrows to your key as well.)

3 'The oxygen produced by the geranium plant diffuses through the air of the greenhouse.' Explain what this means.

4 Digested food diffuses from the small intestine into the blood. Explain what that means and why food diffuses in that direction.

4.2 Understanding osmosis

Keeping the right amount of water inside cells is important and too much is just as bad as too little. For example, if red blood cells are put into pure water they take in water, expand and burst. Roadside plants are often affected by the salt used to de-ice roads. The salty spray from passing cars makes the plants lose water from their cells, so they shrivel up and die.

A simple model can help show how solutions affect cells. A cellophane bag can be used to represent the cell membrane, because the water movement is very like that in a cell. Figure 1 shows what happens when the model is put into a beaker of water.

1 a) Copy Figure 1.
b) Which substance seems to have moved, and in what direction (into or out of the bag)? Draw arrows on your diagram to show this.
c) Which substance does not appear to have moved?
d) A completely **permeable** material lets all substances pass through it. Explain why we say the cellophane bag in this experiment is *selectively* permeable.

2 A cellophane bag filled with 200 g of water was put into a beaker containing 5 g of sugar dissolved in 200 g of water. One hour later 20 g of water had moved out of the bag. Sugar had not moved at all. Draw two diagrams to show the start and finish of the experiment.

3 It is not simply the weight of sugar and water which controls whether water moves. Compare Figures 2 and 3. Which feature of the solutions must be different inside and out if the water is to move?

4 Copy the pictures in Figure 4 and draw arrows on each to show which way water will move.

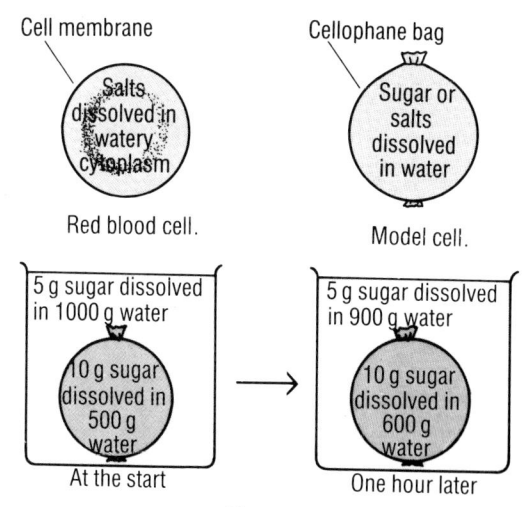

Figure 1.

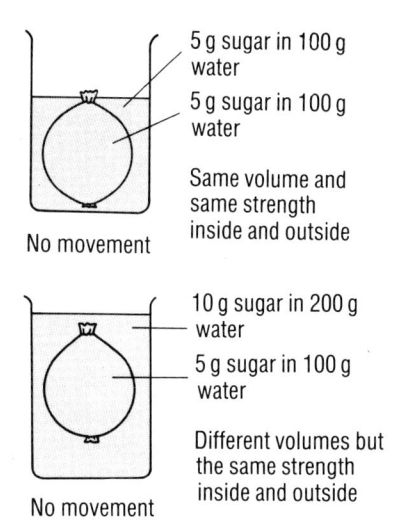

Figure 2.

Figure 3.

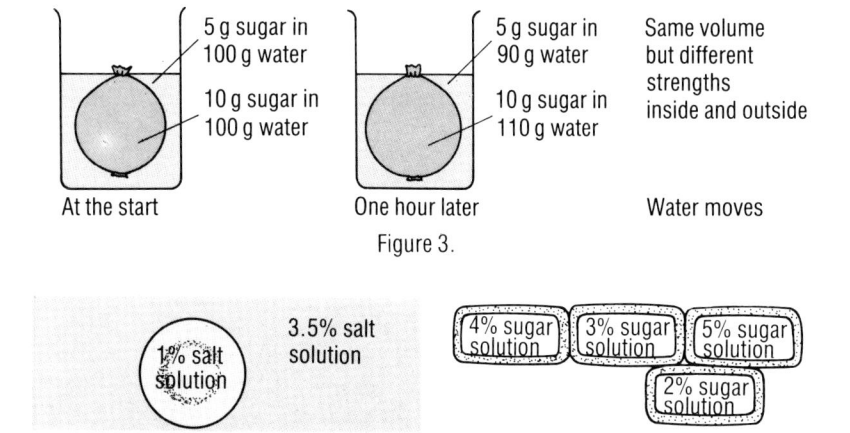

Figure 4.

4.3 The salt marsh environment

A salt marsh with typical plants sea-purslane and sea lavender

In many places round our coasts there are **salt marshes**, which are partly fresh water marsh and partly flooded by the sea. The Ythan estuary, near Aberdeen, and the Wash in England, have large areas of salt marsh. Plants in these areas have to survive very unusual conditions. Sea water, which floods the marsh at high tide, is very salty. As well as the salt problem, the plant roots have to be able to tolerate low oxygen levels when the soil becomes water-logged. Some species have large air spaces in their tissues to store oxygen.

High salinity (salt level) and poor aeration affect the growth of plants, making them small or shrubby. Often the leaves are rounded and fleshy (succulent) to store water when it is readily available for use later. Some leaves have glands to excrete salt if there is too much in the leaf tissue.

Conditions in salt marshes are constantly changing. Tides rise and fall. Heavy rainfall may dilute the salt water. At other times, sun and high winds may increase the evaporation of water, making the salt more concentrated. These changes take place daily, and also with the changing seasons.

A salt marsh is not quite the same everywhere. Conditions in the parts near the sea will be more difficult than in the parts of the marsh that are almost 'dry land'. As some plants can cope better than others, this leads to zonation. (See box.)

Sea aster

Common scurvy grass

Glasswort

Salt marsh plants

Those species which are able to tolerate a high concentration of salt can grow near the salt water, without competition from other species. Less tolerant species can only grow further away from the sea. Two of the factors involved are how well the plants can take up water (see Osmotic potential box) and how well the seeds germinate in salty conditions (see the table). Figure 1 shows the zonation of plants across part of a salt marsh at Keyhaven, Hampshire. The osmotic potential of the cell sap is shown for each species.

Results of germinating seeds in salty water (figures show percentage that germinate)

	Cord grass	Sea aster	Glass-wort	Sea purslane
Tap water	80	45	93	25
1% NaCl	21	25	45	8.3
2% NaCl	15	10	36	0
Sea water	3	0	38	0
5% NaCl	0	0	36	0
10% NaCl	0	0	12	0

Osmotic potential (OP) is a measure of the concentration of cell sap. The higher the osmotic potential, the more concentrated is the cell sap. Salt-tolerant species have special roots to absorb water. The cell sap is more concentrated than sea water so that the plants can take up water by osmosis from the salt water around their roots.

An area showing **zonation** has environmental conditions gradually changing from one extreme to another (like from the water in a pond to the dry land above it). Each of the organisms that lives in the area grows best in one part or zone of the range of conditions so is found mainly in that part.

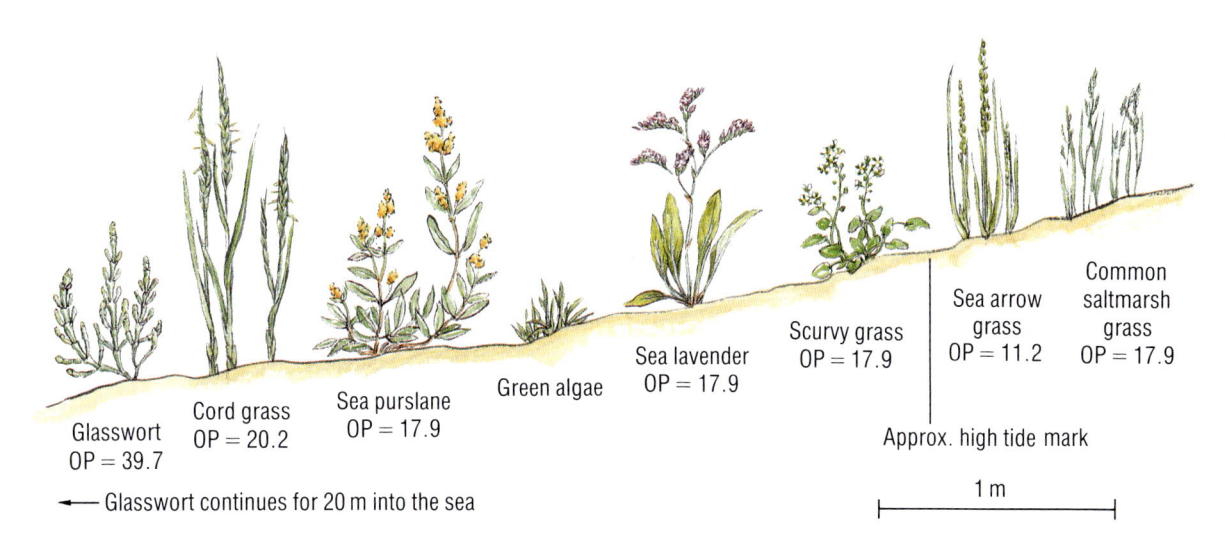

Glasswort OP = 39.7
Cord grass OP = 20.2
Sea purslane OP = 17.9
Green algae
Sea lavender OP = 17.9
Scurvy grass OP = 17.9
Sea arrow grass OP = 11.2
Common saltmarsh grass OP = 17.9

← Glasswort continues for 20 m into the sea
Approx. high tide mark
1 m

Figure 1. Zonation of salt marsh plants.

1 List four adaptations found in salt-tolerant plants and explain how each aids survival in the salt marsh environment.

2 Look at Figure 1.
a) Write down the plants in the order they appear, starting with the one nearest the sea.
b) Use the information about OP to explain the zonation of these plants.

3 Study the table. In which species are the seeds:
a) most tolerant of salt?
b) least tolerant of salt?

4 Explain how your answers to Question 3 match the position of these species in the zonation of salt marsh plants (Figure 1).

5 Sea aster, which appears in the table, is not shown in Figure 1. Between which two species would you expect it to appear in Figure 1?

4.4 Energy use by cells

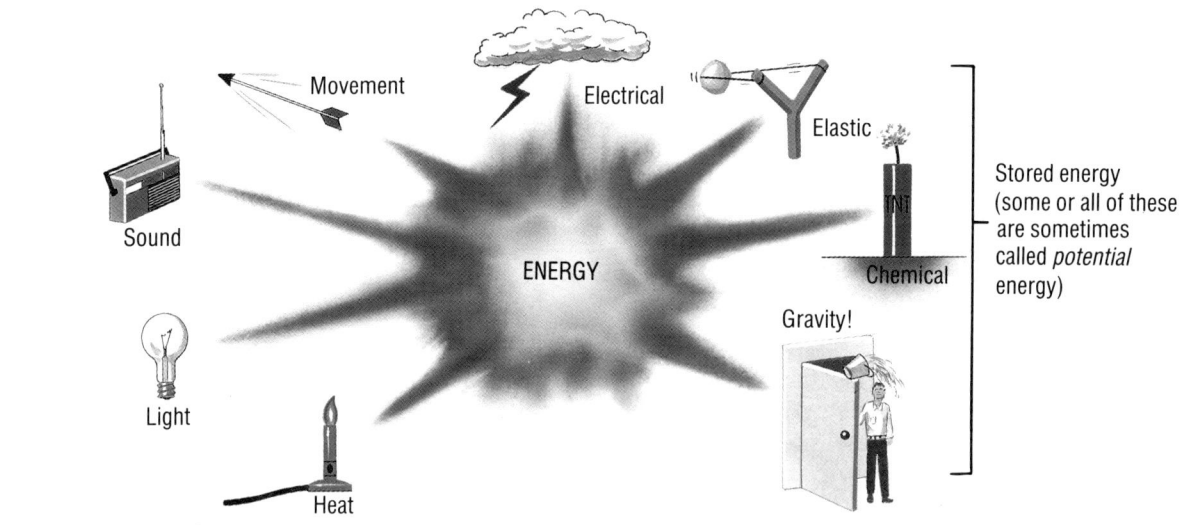

Figure 1. Some forms of energy.

Energy makes things happen. There are many forms of energy (Figure 1).

Energy cannot be destroyed but it can be *changed* from one kind into another. Some forms of energy are more useful for doing work than others. In our homes **electricity** is a convenient source of energy. We put electricity into our transistor radios to give us sound, and into the TV set to get light for making the picture.

In cells, the most convenient source of energy is usually the **chemical energy** stored in foods. This energy is released from the food by respiration. It is changed into other forms for use by the cell. Figure 2 shows some energy changes possible in cells.

The diagrams around the page show some energy changes in cells or in whole organisms.

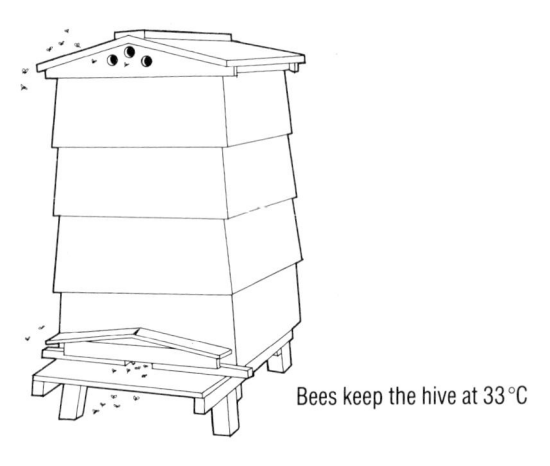

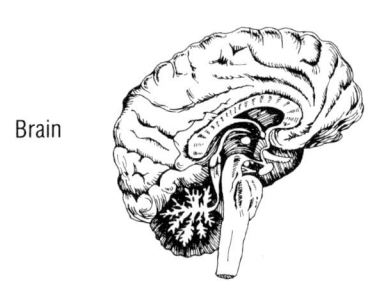

Brain

Electric currents pass messages along projections of nerve cells

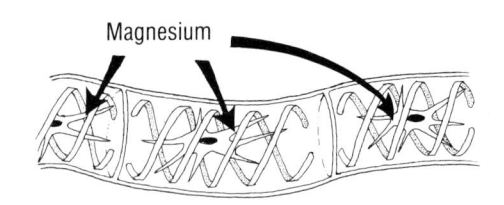

Cells in fresh water 'pull' in minerals

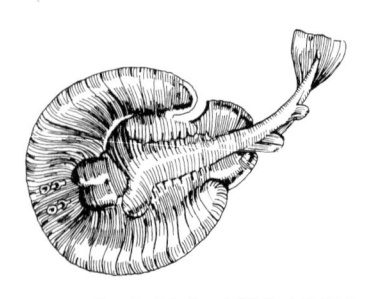

Bees keep the hive at 33 °C

Torpedo ray can make electricity at 50 A at 50 V for a short time

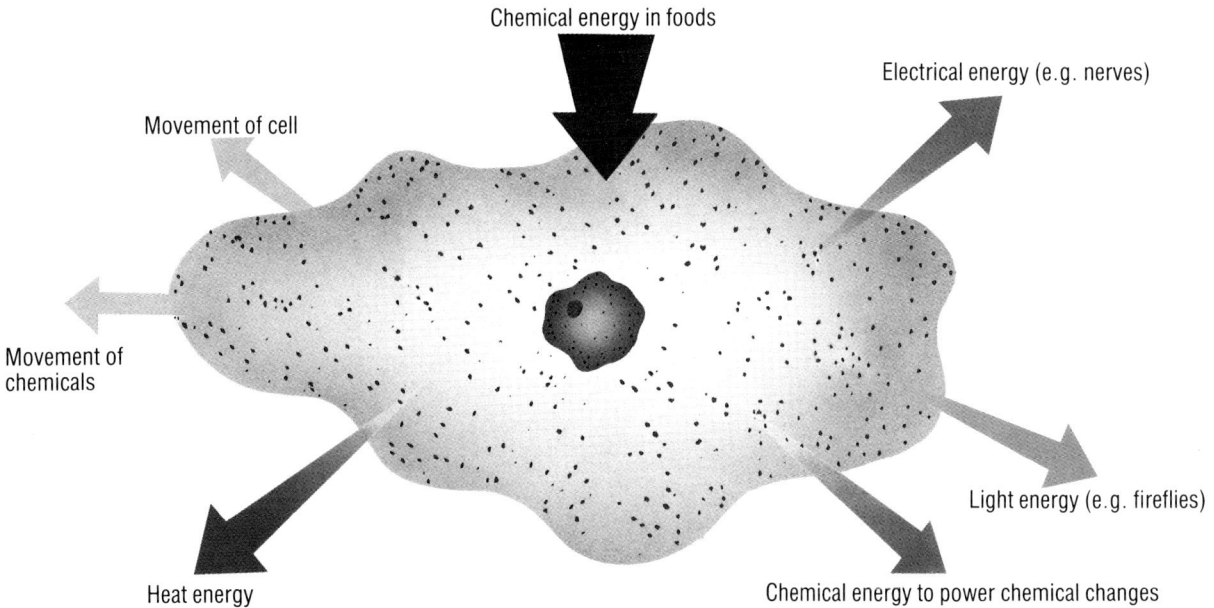

Figure 2. Energy changes in a cell.

Muscle cells make up muscle tissue

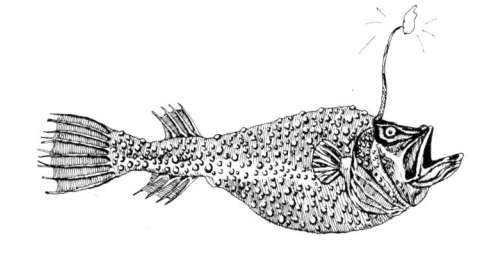

Angler fish in deep oceans show a lighted bait

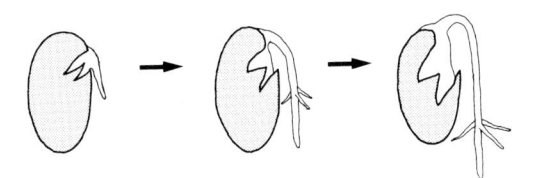

Chemical changes allow cells to grow and divide

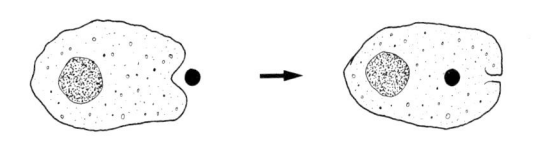

White blood cells move to engulf bacteria

1 What is the main source of energy used by cells?

2 What process makes this energy available to cells?

3 Use the information in Figure 2 and in the small diagrams to make a table showing the kinds of energy change possible in cells and examples of these changes.

4 Green plants have only been shown in a few pictures. They can carry out photosynthesis. What special energy change happens in photosynthesis?

4.5 Give and take

The food we eat contains stored chemical energy. Respiration releases this energy to power the body's activities. Some of the energy is always converted to heat energy. Birds and mammals convert about 80% of their food's energy into heat to keep their bodies warm. Other animals, the so-called 'cold-blooded' ones, like frogs or beetles, produce less heat. Plants produce less still, but some of their food's energy always appears as heat. If an organism is alive, then respiration must be producing some heat inside its body.

If we put heat energy *into* an object it gets hotter. We say its temperature rises. If it *loses* heat, it gets colder and its temperature falls. An object can take in heat and lose heat at the same time. Whether it gets hotter or colder depends on which is greater – the gain or the loss.

The pictures below show the temperature changes caused by heat moving into and out of beakers of water.

Remember – Heat always moves from a hotter object towards a colder object

If heat gained is less than heat lost, the temperature falls

The water is hotter than the air so heat moves out into the air. The water is losing heat so its temperature falls.

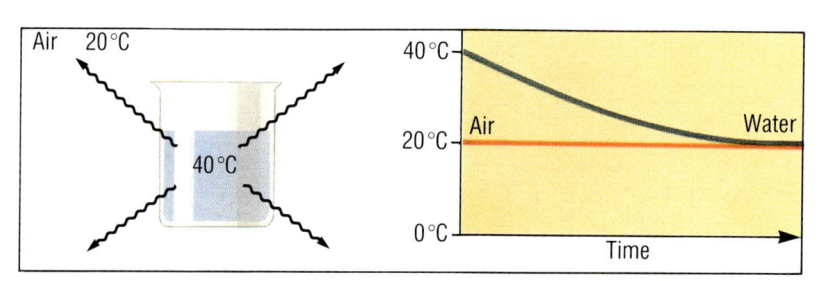

If heat gained is more than heat lost, the temperature rises

The water is hotter than the air and so loses heat to the air. But the water gains more heat from the flame than it loses. The amount of heat gained is *more* than the heat lost so the temperature *rises*.

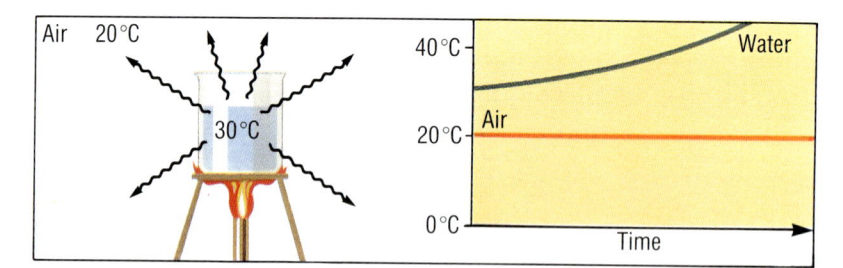

If heat gained is equal to heat lost, the temperature is steady

The water is hotter than the air so heat moves out into the air. The flame adds the same amount of heat as is lost. Heat lost = heat gained. The temperature stays the same.

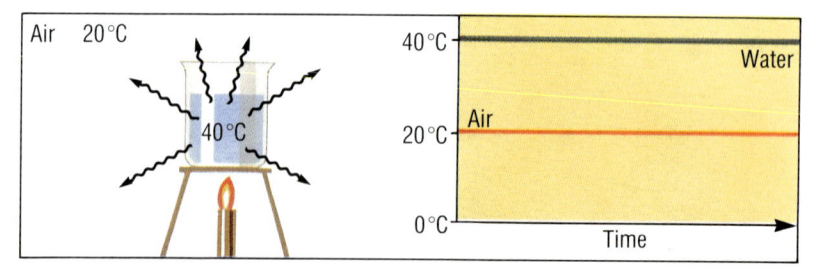

1 **a)** For each of Experiments 1–4 below you should write the experiment number, then draw the picture and graph.
b) Is the animal gaining heat? If so, how?
c) Is the animal losing heat? If so, to where, and why?
d) What change in temperature is happening?
e) Which is greater – heat loss or heat gain?

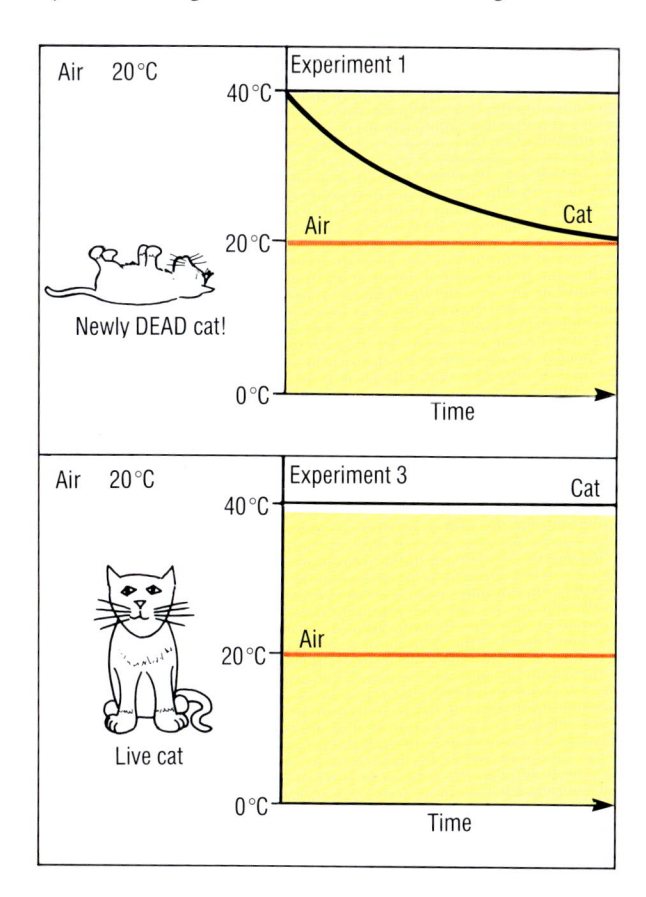

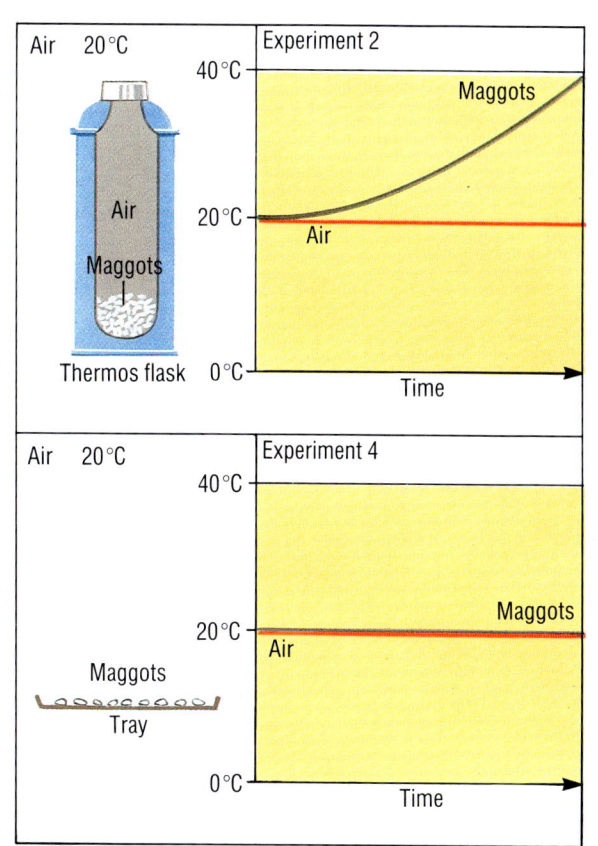

Experiment 1	Experiment 2
Air 20°C — Newly DEAD cat! Graph: Cat cools from 40°C to 20°C (Air line at 20°C)	Air 20°C — Thermos flask with Air/Maggots. Graph: Maggots rise from 20°C toward 40°C (Air line at 20°C)
Experiment 3	Experiment 4
Air 20°C — Live cat. Graph: Cat stays at 40°C (Air line at 20°C)	Air 20°C — Maggots on Tray. Graph: Maggots stay at 20°C (Air line at 20°C)

2 Experiments 5 and 6 are supposed to use temperature changes to show whether worms or maggots respire faster. Each experiment has a mistake in it which makes it unfair. For each one you should say what the mistake is, and explain how the mistake produces the differences in temperatures shown on the graphs.

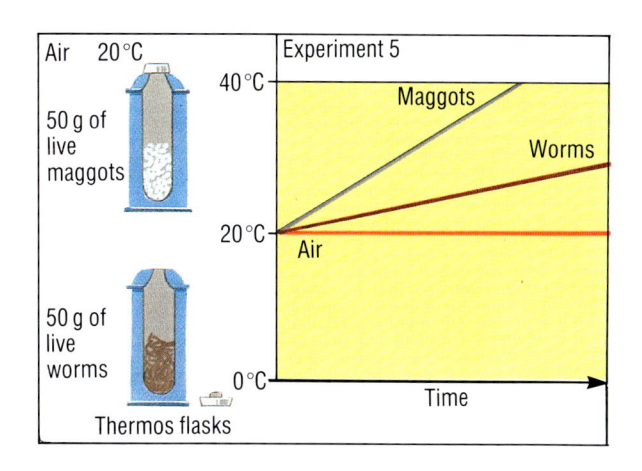

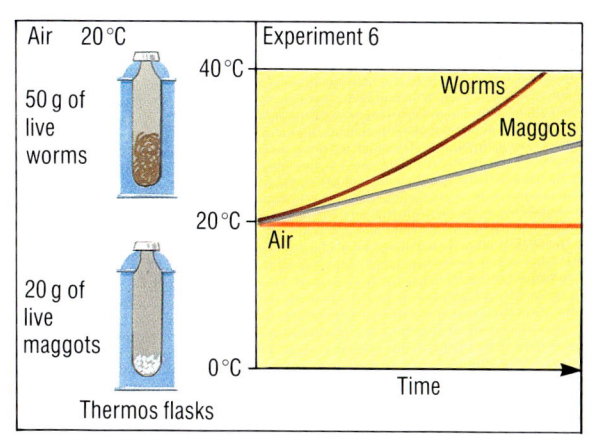

Experiment 5: Air 20°C. Thermos flasks containing 50 g of live maggots and 50 g of live worms. Graph shows Maggots rising steeply, Worms rising gently, Air line at 20°C.

Experiment 6: Air 20°C. Thermos flasks containing 50 g of live worms and 20 g of live maggots. Graph shows Worms rising steeply, Maggots rising less steeply, Air line at 20°C.

57

4.6 Warming up

Temperature has an important influence on the activity of many animals. Lizards are able to move quickly when the weather is hot. Cool weather slows them down. Their muscles can only contract quickly when their temperature is high. Grasshoppers 'sing' on warm days, and other insects are also more active and easily noticed then. But what happens when the weather is not as hot? Many insects just don't move around as much. However, some insects are still active in cool weather. Butterflies do fly on cool days, and most moths fly at night, in fairly cool conditions. These insects often spend time rapidly flapping their wings before they actually take off. The amount of time spent flapping their wings varies with air temperature (see the table).

1 Draw a graph of wing-flapping time against temperature.

2 Predict the wing-flapping time when the air temperature is 26 °C.

3 What do you think the temperature inside the muscles has to be for flight to be possible?

Wing-flapping by red admiral butterfly

Temp. of air	11 °C	18 °C	34 °C	37 °C	40 °C
Wing-flapping time	6 min	1.5 min	18 s	0	0

Could the wing-flapping have something to do with the temperature inside the insect? The temperature inside the thorax and abdomen of a large moth was measured frequently for a period of two hours. The times when the moth flapped its wings were carefully noted. Figure 1 shows where the thorax and abdomen are. Figure 2 shows the results.

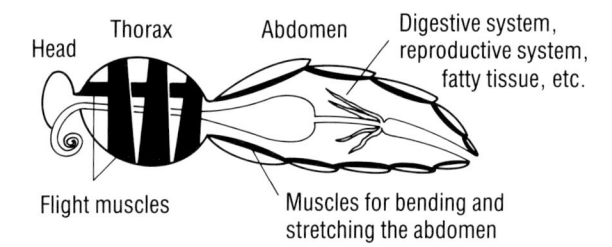

Figure 1. Sectional view of a moth (simplified).

4 Does the graph suggest that warmth allows flapping to happen *or* that flapping causes the temperature to rise?

5 a) What process in the moth's cells produces this heat?
b) Which tissue probably produces most heat?

6 The temperature in the abdomen did not change much. Look at Figure 1 again and suggest reason(s) why.

7 Moths which fly at night are usually furry. How might this help with flight?

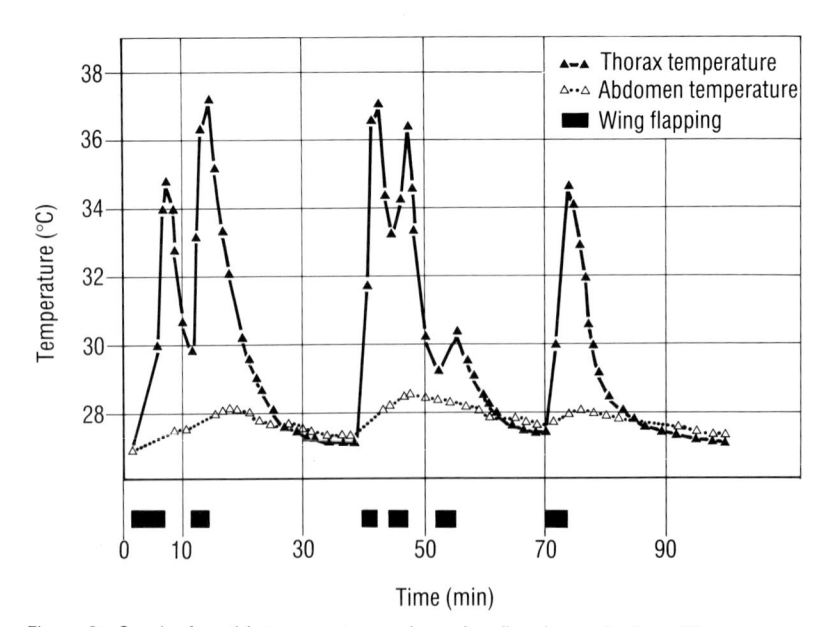

Figure 2. Graph of moth's temperatures when wing-flapping and when still.

4.7 Testing Zoomo

Zoomo is a new 'biological' washing powder promoted by an advertising campaign on TV. The enzymes in it are produced by genetically engineered microbes.

ZOOMO WILL WASH YOUR CLOTHES SUPER-CLEAN!

AND I'LL PROVE IT TO YOU SCIENTIFICALLY!

WE'LL TAKE THESE TWO GARMENTS...

PUT THEM IN TWO SEPARATE WASHING MACHINES.

DIAL UP TWO PROGRAMMES...

AND FINALLY! ADD ZOOMO TO ONE MACHINE, ANY OTHER POWDER TO THE OTHER AND SWITCH ON!!

NOW COMPARE THE TWO GARMENTS!

THIS EXPERIMENT PROVES THAT ZOOMO WASHES YOUR CLOTHES CLEANER THAN ANY OTHER POWDER: THIS IS DUE TO BIOLOGICAL ENZYMES!!

This experiment does not really show that Zoomo washes better than the other washing powder.

1 Give all the reasons why this experiment is unfair. You should be able to think of at least four.

2 The experiment was redesigned to make it fair. This time the garment washed in Zoomo still came out cleaner. Does this prove that it was Zoomo's enzymes which made the difference? Explain your answer.

4.8 Enzymes at work

Living things can survive in an amazing range of conditions, from the icy cold (4°C) of the Polar seas to the blistering heat of volcanic springs (95°C). Wherever they live, all their cells' chemistry is catalysed and controlled by *enzymes*. Each of these enzymes works best at a particular temperature and level of pH.

Many enzymes are now being extracted from organisms, especially from bacteria and fungi, to catalyse chemical processes in industry.

Extreme living conditions.

Starch splitting **amylases** are used to improve the quality of flour for baking and to convert starch solutions to sugar syrups for the food industry.

Pectolases break open the cells in fruit, making it easier to extract the juice.

Protein splitting **proteases** help remove hair from skins in leather manufacture. Others digest the gelatin protein from used photographic film, so the valuable silver salts can be recovered. Proteases are also used in washing powders.

These need enzymes in their production.

Table 1. Activity of amylase Q. Figures show the percentage of starch converted to maltose.

All new enzymes are tested to find out how active they are at different temperatures and pH, that is, how much of their substrate they convert to product in a standard time. Table 1 shows the results of a series of tests on a commercial amylase that converts starch to maltose syrup for use in the brewing industry. The figures show what percentage of the starch is converted to maltose.

pH	3	4	5	6	7	8
Temperature						
40°C	48	67	85	93	81	35
50°C	37	74	89	96	90	52
60°C	7	30	96	98	85	46
65°C	0	7	40	70	74	30
70°C	0	0	30	33	28	7

1 What conditions of temperature and pH give the highest level of activity for this enzyme?

2 Plot a graph to show how changing pH affects the enzyme's activity at this temperature.

3 The best temperature for this enzyme depends on the pH. Plot a graph to show how the optimum temperature is different at different pH levels.

Proteases are used in 'biological' washing powders. They digest and dissolve away difficult stains caused by proteins, such as those in blood, sweat and foods like egg yolk. Which enzyme is best depends on what wash temperature the powder is for, and what pH and other conditions are produced by the other chemicals in the powder. For example, most washing powders contain detergents that make conditions alkaline, around pH 8 or 9.

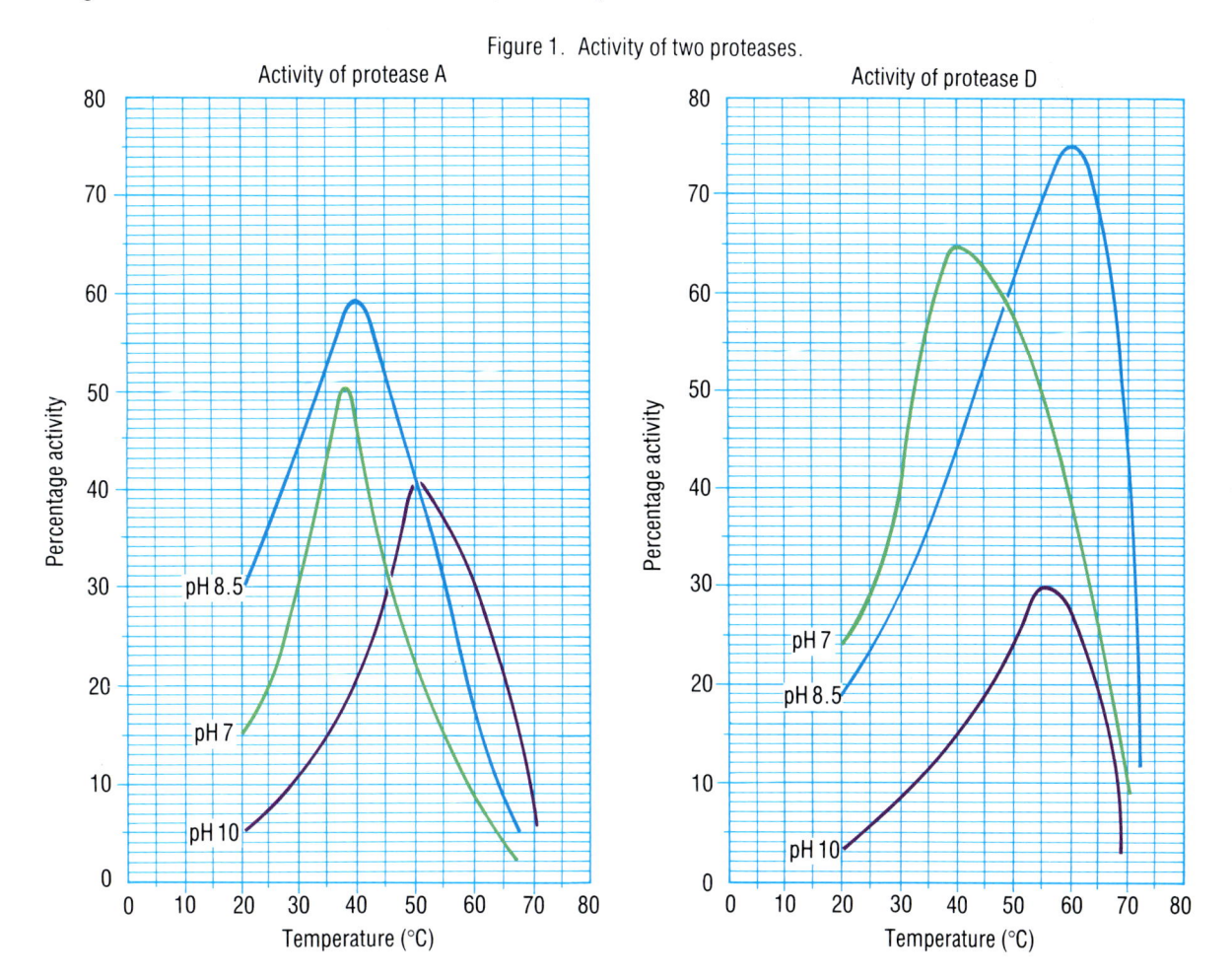

Figure 1. Activity of two proteases.

Look at Figure 1.

4 Make up a table like the one below, to show the activity of the two enzymes at pH 8.5, at different wash temperatures.

	Activity at pH 8.5	
	Protease A	Protease D
Warm (40°C)		
Medium (50°C)		
Hot (60°C)		

All these contain enzymes.

5 Which enzyme would give the maximum activity in a warm wash?

6 a) Which enzyme would be best to use for a hot wash?
b) Would this still be the best enzyme to use if pH conditions were neutral?

7 a) Explain why it is surprising that 'biological' washing powders still work at 85–90°C.
b) How *do* they work at this temperature?

61

5.1 Input = output?

Your body uses energy in moving around, and in keeping itself warmer than the environment. Energy is also used in less obvious ways, such as movement of substances into and out of cells. New tissue produced by growth has energy stored in its chemicals. Where do we get all this energy from? From our food, of course. But how much energy is used, and for what? How much energy is contained in the food eaten? We need the answers to these questions to make a 'balance sheet' of energy intake and use.

To allow them to make these energy measurements, biologists have built special cages, or even rooms! (see Figure 1).

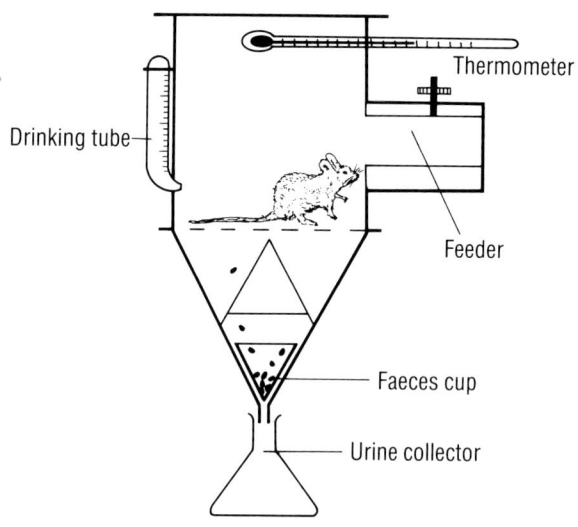

Figure 1.
A 'metabolic cage'. Measurements are made of the heat given out by the vole, the weight of food it eats, and the weights, temperatures and energy remaining in the wastes it produces. Any gain in weight counts as extra energy stored in its body.

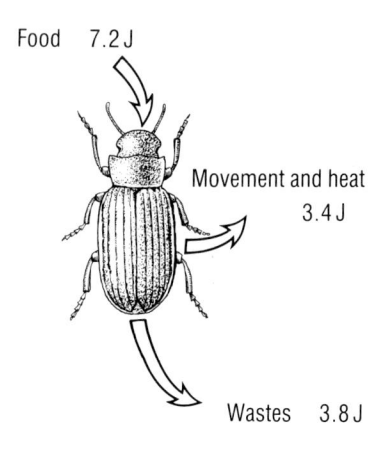

Figure 2. Daily balance of *Tribolium* beetle.

Food 7.2 J
Movement and heat 3.4 J
Wastes 3.8 J

Energy data sheet
Species: Bank vole
Dates: 15/1 → 20/1
Initial weight: 24.5 g
Final weight: 24.5 g
Food: Beech mast

Item	kJ	Percentage
Food	313	100
Faeces	21.9	7.0
Urine	9.8	3.2
Heat and movement	281.3	89.8

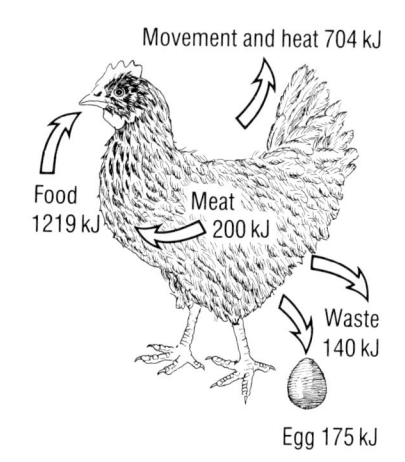

Figure 3. Daily balance of a laying hen, weighing 2 kg.

Movement and heat 704 kJ
Food 1219 kJ
Meat 200 kJ
Waste 140 kJ
Egg 175 kJ

1 Does the energy that the *Tribolium* beetle (Figure 2) takes in equal the energy that it gives out?

Look at the table. Bank voles are small rodents about the same size as field mice. The vole was being studied in a 'metabolic cage' like the one in Figure 1.

2 a) What was the vole eating?
b) Had the vole changed its weight at the end of the experiment?
c) Draw an 'energy balance diagram' (like the one for the beetle) for the vole. Put the kilojoules and the percentages on it.

Look at Figure 3.

3 Compare the hen's food energy intake with its energy losses.

4 What percentage of the hen's food intake is turned into 'new chicken body or product' which could eventually be eaten by people?

5 Look at all the diagrams. Write a summary statement comparing energy input with output in all these organisms.

6 If an animal were starving how would you expect input to compare with output?

5.2 Pick a packed lunch

If you go to the shops on Saturday, buy enough food to last until Wednesday, but then run out of food on Tuesday, it isn't the end of the world. You can nip into the shops for some more. In normal life, planning out your food consumption doesn't demand accurate knowledge of exactly how much you need, and it does not matter if you get it wrong. It *does* matter in some cases. There have been cases when it was a life or death matter, for example on polar expeditions.

It is possible to measure the amount of energy in foods and to measure the energy used in various activities, such as walking and running. This means you can work out how much of a particular food will give enough energy for a particular activity.

This mountaineer carries all the food he will need on his back.

Figure 1. Foods to choose from.

Foods shown with energy values:
- SUGAR 100 kJ
- TEA with MILK 70 kJ
- LOW CAL DRINKS 10 kJ
- HONEY 680 kJ
- BUTTER 420 kJ
- LEMONADE 420 kJ
- CAKE 500 kJ
- BANANA 460 kJ
- BREAD 260 kJ
- CHEESE 460 kJ
- BOILED EGG 380 kJ
- CHOCOLATE 1300 kJ
- APPLE 380 kJ
- ORANGE 300 kJ

Table 1. Energy expenditure of some activities

Activity	Energy requirement (kJ/hour)
Lying down	260
Sitting	288
Standing	360
Normal walking	1300
Fast walking up hill	3600

Table 2. Timetable for morning

9.00	Assemble (stand about)
9.15	Set off, walking to base of hill
10.15	Race up hill (walking only)
10.45	Rest (sitting)
11.00	Walk on gentle slope to summit
12.00	Lunch

1 How long will the energy in one slice of bread last you while you are:
a) lying down?   b) walking normally?

2 Imagine that you are going to spend a day hill-walking. Use Table 1 and the timetable for the morning (Table 2) to work out how much energy you use between 9.00 and 12.00.

Figure 1 shows some portions of food laid out, each with its energy content. Imagine that this was the choice that was provided for people to make up their own packed lunches.

3 You are to choose a packed lunch that will replace the energy used in the morning to within 40kJ more or less.
a) Working in rough, list the lunch items.
b) Beside each food write its energy value and check that the total is what it should be.
c) Make any corrections and then copy the information into your notebook.

5.3 Weight watchers

Most of us know someone who has 'been on a diet'. They have changed what they ate, usually to try to lose weight. Unfortunately fewer than 20% of dieters actually manage to keep their weight down. Most put it all back on again very quickly.

Why don't 'slimming diets' seem to work? To understand this we need to know how our body reacts to a reduction in 'energy foods' like sugars and starch or fat.

Normally, the energy in food should exactly balance the energy given out.

People who eat *more* energy food than they use up put their 'energy equation' out of balance. The extra, unused food is converted to fat and stored, much of it just under the skin. To lose fat, they must unbalance their energy equation in the other direction. The energy in their food must be less than that used up. They must either eat *less*, or use more energy, perhaps by taking more exercise.

Slimming diets depend on the dieter eating less. The idea is that the diet forces the body to 'burn up' its stores of fat, to provide the person with enough energy for normal daily activity.

If it were as simple as this, cutting out 200 kJ a day (just one digestive biscuit!) would force your body to burn up about 5g of body fat a day. This may not seem much but it ought to add up to almost 2 kg in a year. Cutting out a Mars bar a day (1000 kJ) would lose a dieter 10 kg a year.

As Figure 1 shows, what actually happens to the body during a diet is more complicated.

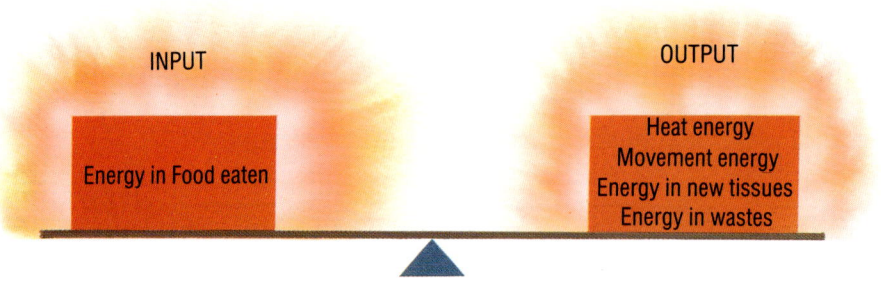

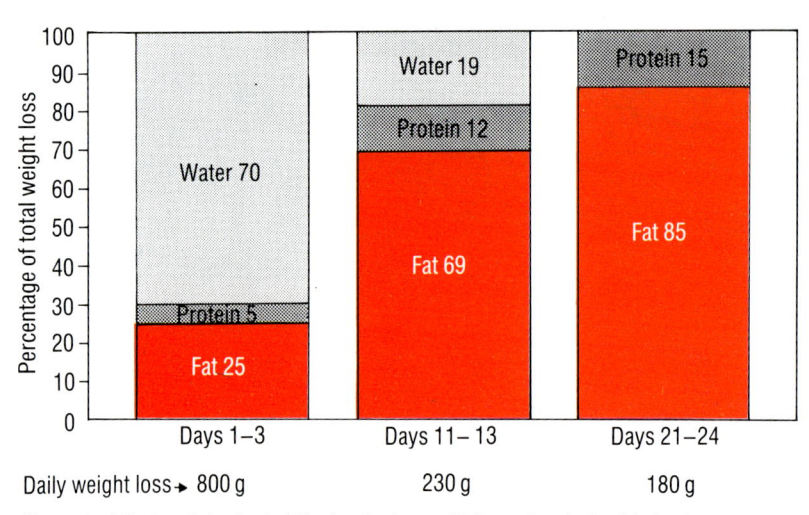

Figure 1. What a dieter lost at the beginning, middle and end of a 24-day low-energy diet (4000 kJ per day).

Daily weight loss → 800 g (Days 1–3), 230 g (Days 11–13), 180 g (Days 21–24)

1 What three kinds of material were lost from the body?

2 What was the *total* weight loss over days 1–3?

3 What percentage was fat, and how many grams is this?

4 What made up most of the first 3 days' weight loss?

5 What was the *total* weight loss over days 11–13?

6 What percentage is fat, and how many grams is this?

7 What happens to the amount of weight lost per day as the diet goes on?

8 What happens to the percentage of loss that is *fat*?

9 Most loss in days 21–24 was fat. What was the rest?

Crash-diets that last for just a few days, less than a week, lose mostly water, and a starch-like food store called glycogen. This loss is very quickly replaced when the diet stops. Only longer term diets cause much fat loss. It is important to notice that *protein* is always lost during a diet. Much of this protein is active, energy-using muscle. This means that the dieter's body tends to be less able to use up energy after the diet.

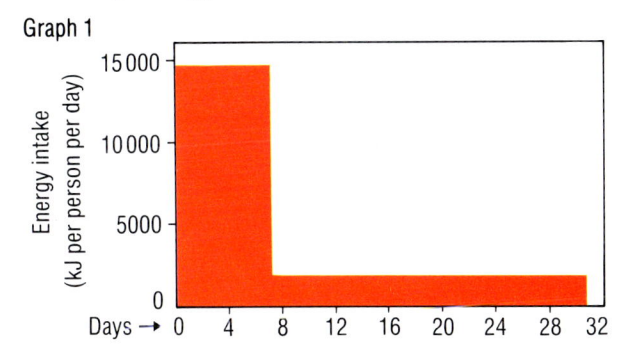

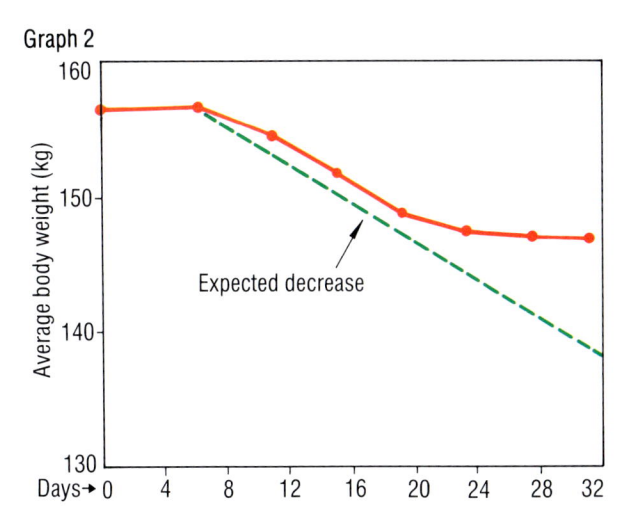

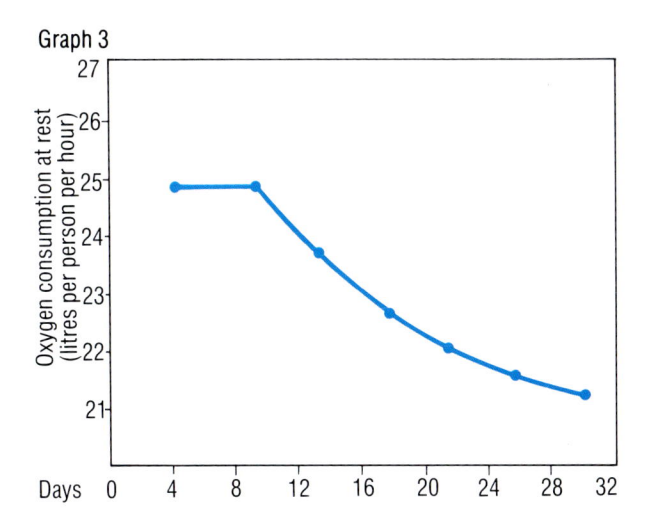

Graph 1
(Energy intake, kJ per person per day, vs Days 0–32)

Graph 2
(Average body weight (kg) vs Days 0–32, with "Expected decrease" dashed line)

Graph 3
(Oxygen consumption at rest, litres per person per hour, vs Days 0–32)

Figure 2. Three graphs showing intake, body weight and oxygen use during a near-starvation diet (1800 kJ per day).

Figure 2 shows the results of an experiment on a group of six overweight men.

During the first 7 days of the experiment they each ate 14 500 kJ per day. For the remaining 24 days they cut their intake to a near-starvation level of 1800 kJ each per day. Their food intake, their body weight and their oxygen use at rest were carefully checked each day.

10 What happened to the men's body weight during the first 7 days?

11 What does this tell you about their energy-balance when eating 14 500 kJ each per day?

12 The dotted line on graph 2 shows the weight loss expected as a result of their diet (50 g loss per day for each 2000 kJ cut out). Describe how well the actual loss fitted the prediction.

13 a) Look at graph 3. What changes in oxygen consumption happened during the experiment?
b) Oxygen consumption gives a measure of rate of respiration, that is, of how fast food is burned up. What happened to the men's rate of food-burning when they started dieting?
c) How does this explain their rate of weight loss?

14 a) Describe their rate of food burning at the end of the experiment, compared with the rate at the start.
b) What change in body composition has most probably caused this?

15 Say what seems likely to happen to the body weight of these men if they return to their original diet of 14 500 kJ each per day after the end of the experiment.

5.4 Breathing bad air

'Second hand air' is used to fill the lungs of an accident victim by the 'kiss of life'. Yet, as Table 1 shows, this air is *not* the same as normal fresh air.

Table 1. Comparing the composition of different air samples

	Normal air, unbreathed	Breathed air
Oxygen	21%	17%
Carbon dioxide	0.04%	4%
Nitrogen	79%	79%

Tilting the victim's head well back makes sure the airway is clear. The donor's air is breathed out straight into the victim's lungs.

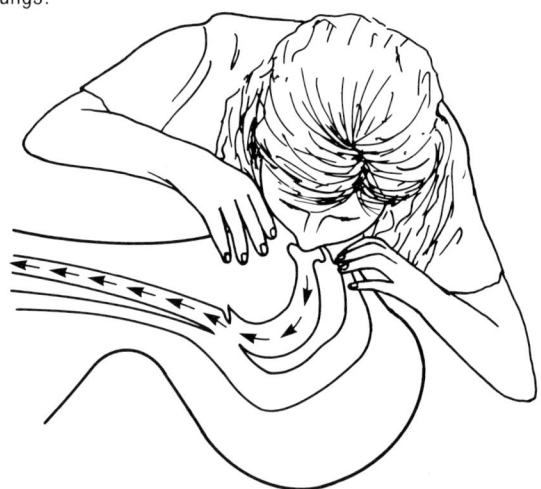

Cut-away diagram of victim's head to show air passages.

1 Draw a diagram to show the differences between breathed and unbreathed air as shown in Table 1. Choose the best kind of diagram.

2 What does Table 1 or your diagram tell you about:
a) the use of nitrogen in the body?
b) the use of oxygen in the body?
c) the use of carbon dioxide in the body?

3 How does this explain why 'second hand air' is still of use to accident victims?

Experiments on the effects of changing the air breathed have been done on animals. When a rabbit is breathing normal air it takes 72 breaths per minute and the volume of each breath is 19 cm³. In one set of experiments two levels of increased carbon dioxide were used: 4.2% CO_2 and 8.6% CO_2. In the first experiment the rabbit increased its rate of breathing to 96 breaths per minute with a volume of 25 cm³ per breath. In the second experiment the figures were 97 breaths per minute and 29 cm³.

Percentage CO_2	Breaths per minute	Volume of each breath (cm³)	Total air volume per minute	Extra air volume per minute	Percentage increase
				–	–

4 Copy the table below and write the results of the rabbit experiments in the first three columns. Give the table a title.

5 Calculate the total volume of air taken in per minute in each of the three conditions. Add these figures to your table.

6 a) For each of the two high CO_2 conditions work out how much *more* air is breathed per minute than in normal air.
b) Calculate the *percentage* increases these are. Put all these figures on your table.

7 Suggest two reasons why the total volume of air per minute does not rise much in the last experiment.

When changes really matter

Submarines are airtight, for obvious reasons. There is not much space inside, and there are large numbers of people living and working in them, using up the oxygen and adding carbon dioxide to the air. The crew depend on air purification systems to prevent these changes from having serious effects. In 1939 the submarine HMS Thetis sank while still on sea trials. It was thought that the decreasing oxygen level and increasing carbon dioxide level might have affected the crew's ability to think and act in a logical and co-ordinated way. This could explain why 99 men died, despite all the escape equipment carried in the vessel.

The graphs in Figure 1 show how human breathing rates change when the gases breathed in are altered. Each graph shows a three minute period when the gas breathed was changed from normal.

Devotion to duty!
J.B.S. Haldane and a colleague – trapped in a diving bell above Portsmouth Harbour during an air raid. They were trying to find out how high levels of CO_2 affected their breathing rates.

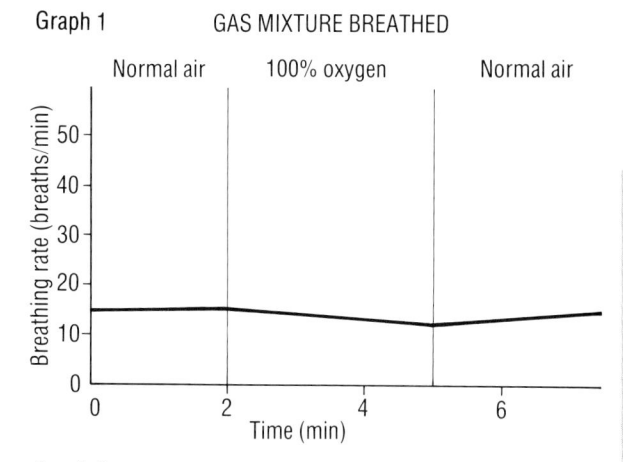

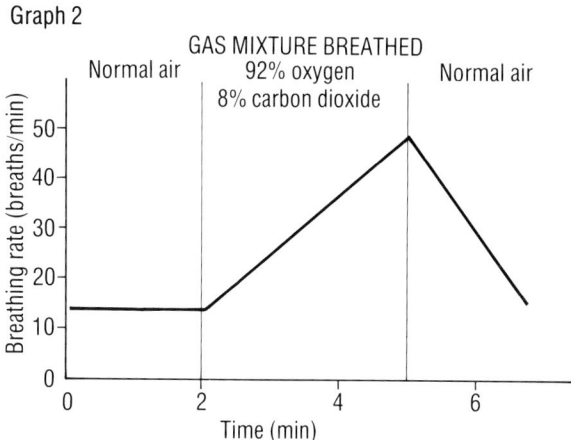

Figure 1. Effects of changing composition of gas breathed in.

8 From graph 1, what does extra oxygen do to the breathing rate?

9 In graph 2, is the percentage of oxygen between 2 and 5 minutes more or less than is found in normal air?

10 'The high oxygen level in graph 2 is *not* the cause of the increased rate of breathing'. What evidence is there in graph 1 for this statement?

11 What has caused the increased rate of breathing in graph 2?

12 Imagine you are going to design an air purification system for a place where there may be many people working in an enclosed space.
a) If the place was only likely to be sealed from the outside during short-term emergencies, which would you think more important, an oxygen addition system or a carbon dioxide removal system? Give reasons for your answer.
b) Why would the answer that you gave for **a)** not be true if you were designing a system which had to purify air for a long time, not merely in a short-term emergency?

5.5 Actively healthy?

Are there rules for staying healthy? Do we know, for example, what causes heart disease? In human populations it is often quite difficult to *prove* something for certain. People *differ* in many ways. They have different diets, occupations, personalities and levels of activity. They inherit different genes from their parents. All these things may have to be taken into consideration when you are trying to find the best way to avoid a heart attack.

Here are two investigations of the relationship between diet, exercise and problems in the heart and arteries. Your task is to look *critically* at both and decide what they tell us. Are they fair comparisons? What do they actually show? What information is missing? How could you be more sure that the results really show something useful about heart disease?

Kramsch's monkeys

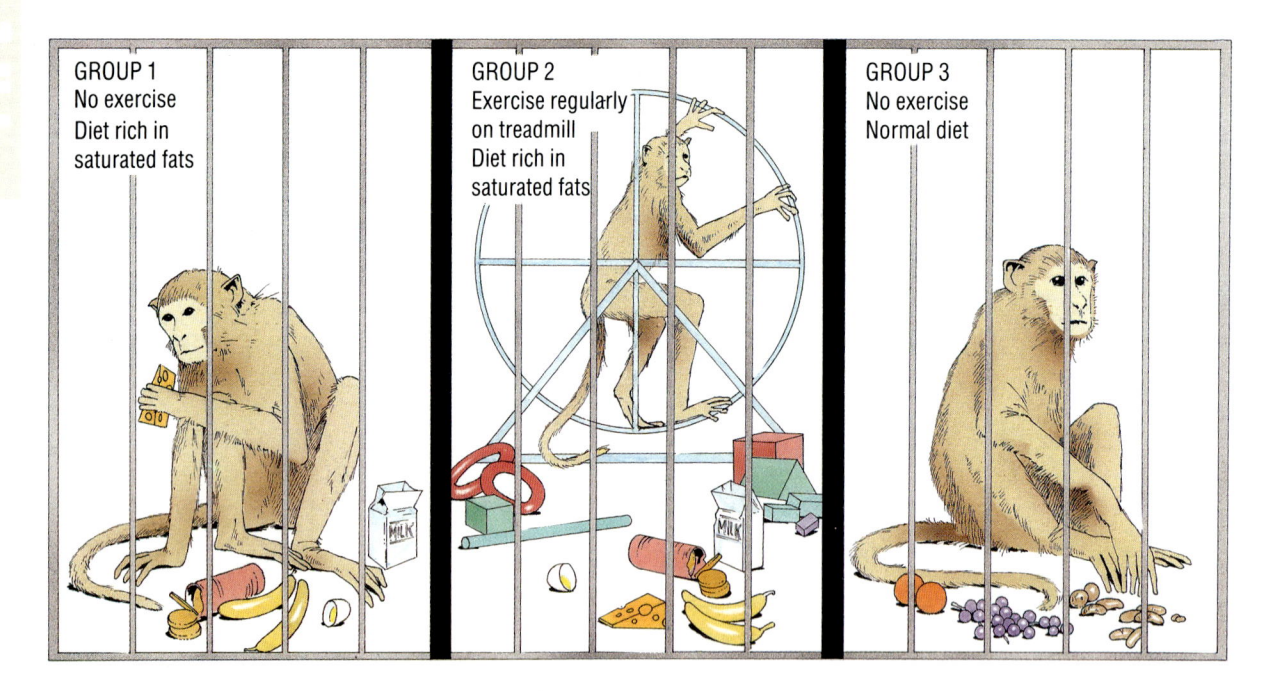

GROUP 1
No exercise
Diet rich in saturated fats

GROUP 2
Exercise regularly on treadmill
Diet rich in saturated fats

GROUP 3
No exercise
Normal diet

Kramsch carried out an experiment which many people would regard as inhumane. He studied 27 young Macaque monkeys which he divided into three groups of nine.

Although the monkeys were studied over a period of three years, the exercise on the treadmill was only introduced after 18 months. At the end of the three years the whole population was killed, and post-mortems were carried out to examine the hearts and blood vessels. It was assumed that the results could be applied to humans, and that the treadmill would represent jogging exercise.

The arteries of group 1 were clearly hardened and had a narrow cavity due to 'furring' caused by the high fat diet. Both of these changes make it harder for the blood to circulate. The arteries of group 2 were less affected.

Morris's study of London transport workers

This study was completed in 1953, at a time when buses and underground trains had a driver, whose job was mainly sitting still, and conductors and guards who spent most of their working shifts being much more active. The conductors collected fares from the upper and lower decks of buses, while the guards moved around the trains checking equipment, handling goods and dealing with any problems that arose.

Information was collected on 31 000 men between the ages of 35 and 64. The men were not interviewed, however, and all the information was taken from company records.

The survey claimed to show that drivers were fatter than conductors because, on average, the uniform trousers issued to them were 2.5 cm larger around the waist.

Conductors had only half as many heart attacks as drivers, and were also more likely to recover. In addition, conductors who did develop heart disease tended to be affected later in life than drivers, and their illness was, on average, less severe.

1 For each study, say what it suggests people can do to reduce the risk of having a heart attack.

2 For each study, suggest as many reasons as you can why it is hard to say that the results were conclusive proof of a way of preventing heart attacks.
Evidence: Is it complete? What is missing?
Variables: What could be confusing the results?

5.6 I hurt it playing

People who take part in any physical activity run the risk of hurting themselves. No one is surprised that young children have scabby knees, and these minor injuries do not make anyone stop them from going out to play.

Surveys show that most injuries to rugby players are reported after the summer holidays when training restarts. Sports people are usually advised to get fit before trying to do anything very strenuous, so that injuries are less likely. Building up and maintaining fitness demands that you exercise regularly. 'Warming up' before starting to play a match or run a race is another safety measure. You often see athletes doing warm-up exercises to loosen their muscles and increase their circulation.

Young children trip when running about. This means that they most often have grazes on their knees, hands and elbows, as they land on them. The most frequent injuries in different sports are also predictable. People who fall off horses often land on their heads. Even hard hats are not protection enough, although the number of serious injuries is small. Skiers tend to break their legs. One study quotes 500 000 ski injuries per year, 72% of them to 'lower limbs'. These figures sound alarming but really do not say enough. If they said how many skiers were involved, you could calculate how many skiers have no injuries at all, even after hours of sport.

1 What information would you need to be able to compare which has more risk of injury, hockey or shinty?

2 What can people do to reduce the risk of sports injuries?

3 In your head, or on scrap paper, match each drawing of a sport first with the descriptions on the opposite page of the types of activity involved, and then with the diagram showing the numbers and sites of injuries.

4 a) Draw a table as shown below.
b) Put in the names of the sports and copy the correct 'sites of injury' diagram.
c) Complete the table by putting +s in the 'causes' column to show what the cause of damage is likely to be.

Name of sport	Diagram of sites	Cause of damage		
		Equipment	Falls	Twists

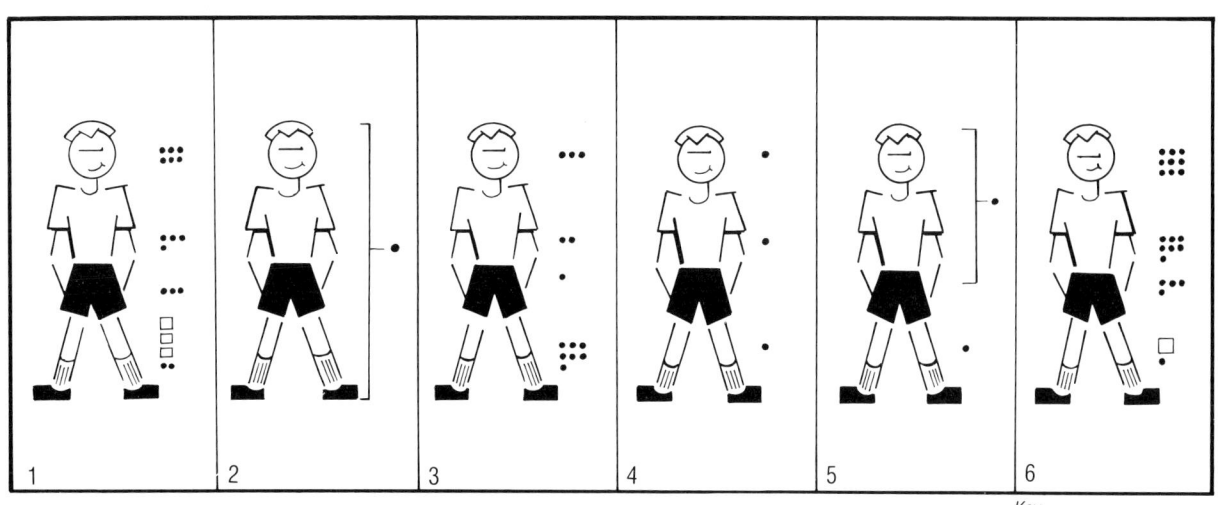

Diagrams to show sites and numbers of injuries.

Key
• = 1 injury per 10 000 person hours of play
▫ = 10 injuries per 10 000 person hours of play

Descriptions

A Good all over movement. Weight very well supported so that injury is uncommon. For this reason often recommended for people recovering from injuries caused by accidents.

B Requires fast movements and neat turns in a small space. Arms and shoulders stretched by reaching for hits. Racket may accidentally hit partner.

C Vigorous contact sport where players deliberately throw each other to the ground. Falls are often on shoulders. Twists involve leg strength.

D Played by hitting small hard ball with a stick. Stress on knees, shins and ankles by sharp turns and changes of speed. Players may edge opponents away from ball, but deliberate use of stick on players is a foul.

E Ball obtained from opponent by knocking him over. Special feature – groups of players hold on to each other and push opposing team away, to get the ball from the centre. Also many sharp turns and changes of speed.

F Fast moving ball game. Players must change direction quickly, which puts strong forces on lower legs, and also may cause falls. Ball is kicked or, more rarely, headed.

THE BODY IN ACTION

71

5.7 Get a grip

In climbing it matters how long you can keep up a powerful grip – otherwise you might fall off before you reached your next 'hold'!
The strength of a person's handgrip is measured by a special handgrip dynamometer like the one shown in Figure 1.

A climber tried to squeeze as steadily as possible for 60 seconds using *one-quarter* of his maximum strength. The dynamometer reading was checked every 5 seconds. In later experiments he tried 60 seconds at *half* strength and then 60 seconds at his absolute *maximum* strength.

The graphs in Figure 2 show how well he did.

1 Describe what happened to his grip strength during the 60 seconds of Experiment 1.

2 What happened when he tried to keep up half strength for a full minute?

If we work muscle fairly hard something happens to stop it working properly. We say the muscle is fatigued.

3 What difference does it make to muscle fatigue if the climber works at maximum strength?

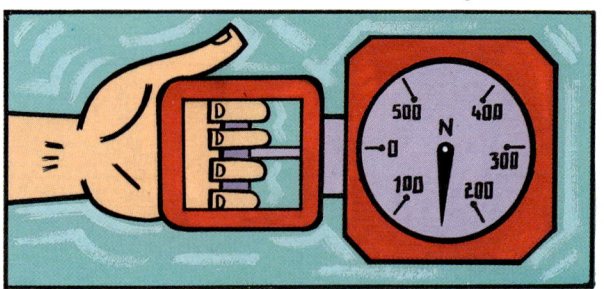

Figure 1.
Gripping the handle stretches a powerful spring. The greater the force the more the spring stretches. The force produced can be read off the scale.

Figure 2. Results of the climber's experiment.

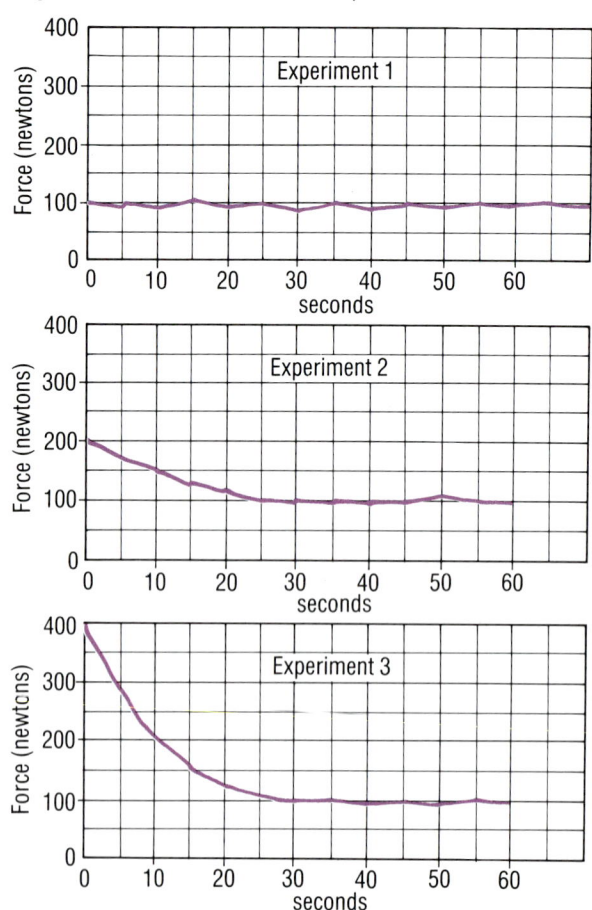

Strengthening muscles

Climbers can strengthen their forearm muscles by repeatedly squeezing a tennis ball or a special spring-grip.

The table shows the *maximum* force produced at the start of a four week period of 'squeeze-training', and at the *end* of each of the next six weeks.

4 In which week did grip strength improve *most*?

5 What happened in the fourth week?

6 Look at the results at the end of the fifth and sixth weeks. What is the result of stopping training?

Results of squeeze training

Week	Force (newtons)	
Start	400	
1	450	
2	490	Training
3	500	
4	500	
5	480	
6	460	

What training is best?

If any of our muscles is not used for a long time, perhaps after an accident, it becomes weak and wastes away. A physiotherapist can design a special training programme to bring our muscles back to full strength as soon as possible.

Accident victims need to have the right size of weight to work against to produce a steady increase in muscle strength. Athletes and weight lifters, too, can improve their strength best by carefully planned training.

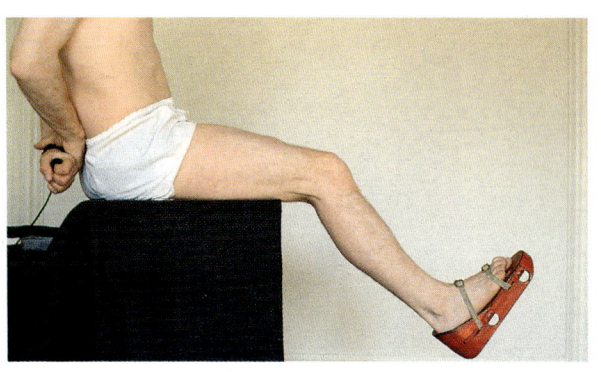

Repeated exercise, lifting this physiotherapy 'shoe', strengthens the thigh muscles. As the patient regains strength, more weight can be added so that the exercise does not become too easy.

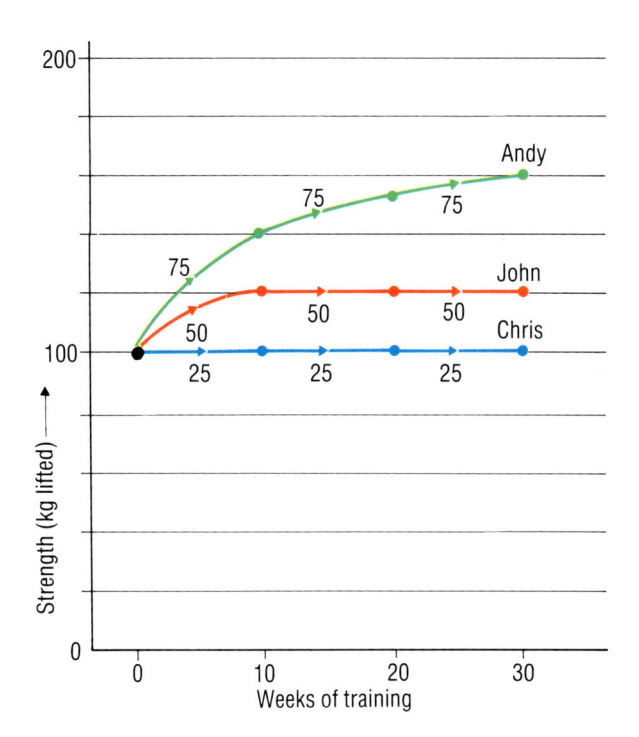

Look at Figure 3.

7 What happened to Chris, who trained with 25 kg?

8 John trained with 50 kg.
a) What happened to his maximum strength over the first 10 weeks?
b) What happened from week 10 to week 30, and why?

9 Andy trained with 75 kg, which is 75% of his original maximum load. Training loads of 75% of maximum are often used, since they produce a very rapid increase in strength.
a) What happened to Andy's maximum strength over the first 10 weeks?
b) What happened to his *rate* of improvement over weeks 10–30, and why?
c) What change could be made in Andy's training so that he would keep up his early rapid rate of improvement?

10 Write a short summary of the main point being made in each of the three main parts of these two pages.

Figure 3.
All these fit young weight lifters could just lift 100 kg at the start of the experiment. Each trained with a different weight, and they all had their maximum possible lift measured at the end of each week.

5.8 More power to your heart

A healthy heart can meet any demand that the body puts on it, from lifting heavy furniture to sprinting for a bus. An unfit heart may become diseased or even suffer a heart attack and stop. *Heart disease really matters.* It may make a person have to give up their job or even die years too soon.

How does the heart meet extra demands?

1 Use the figures from the table to draw two line graphs on the *same* axes showing how pulse rate and volume per beat change with work load.

2 When a person works harder what main changes happen to their heart rate and their heart's output per beat?

3 Describe what happens to both pulse rate and output per beat in two parts of the graph:
a) between A and B, where work load is light.
b) between C and D, where work load is becoming very heavy.

4 Would you say this heart is working well at a pulse rate of 150 beats per minute? Give a reason for your answer.

The heart is like a bag of muscle that keeps steadily pumping blood. The 'bag' can change its size, so that the volume of blood pumped per beat varies. The muscle can be fit or unfit; able to work fast or easily tired.

Pat is an athlete with a resting heart rate of 60 beats per minute. Chris takes no exercise at all, and has a resting heart rate of 80 beats per minute.

Both need 4800 cm^3 of blood to be pumped from their left ventricles every minute when they are at rest.

5 a) Calculate the output per beat of each.
b) When Pat and Chris went jogging together their increased activity meant that they each needed 10 000 cm^3 of blood per minute. At what rate would each heart have to beat? (Assume that in this case output per beat does not change.)
c) Say who would be able to do this exercise more easily, and explain why.

Changes in pulse rate and volume per beat with increasing work

Work (W)	Pulse rate (beats/min)	Volume per beat (cm^3)
40	100	80
A 50	100	84
60	100	92
70	104	100
B 80	106	105
100	108	122
120	110	130
C 140	118	132
150	124	130
160	132	128
D 170	142	127
180	155	125

Training your heart

Here he comes, flying down the street! Big flat feet pounding on the pavement, bright red cheeks puffed out, gasping and wheezing fit to burst, stomach bouncing up and down and eyes popping out of his head! Big Jim is running for the bus!

He grabs the handrail and heaves his bulk aboard. After paying his fare, he bustles along the passage clutching at his collar, and collapses into a seat, mopping his brow with a handkerchief. Another narrow escape from a heart attack!

'My word!' he wheezes to himself. 'I'll have to do something about getting myself fitter before I do that again!'

Can exercise or training bring about an improvement?

The graphs show the results of some experiments on trained and untrained people.

Look at Figure 1.

1 Which group has the lowest heart rate at zero exercise?

2 Which group can exercise hardest?

3 In which group does the heart rate increase fastest with more exercise?

4 In which group is the heart rate least affected by an exercise level of '2'?

5 What are the effects of training on:
a) heart rate at any particular work level?
b) maximum possible work level?

Look at Figure 2.

6 In which group is the volume per beat greatest at rest?

7 What evidence is there that volume per beat is improved by training?

From all the information, answer these questions.

8 After running for a bus, a fit person would recover more quickly than someone who never exercised. Give as many reasons for this as you can.

9 Write a letter to your head teacher explaining why the whole school, staff and students, should spend from 9.00 to 9.20 each morning jogging.

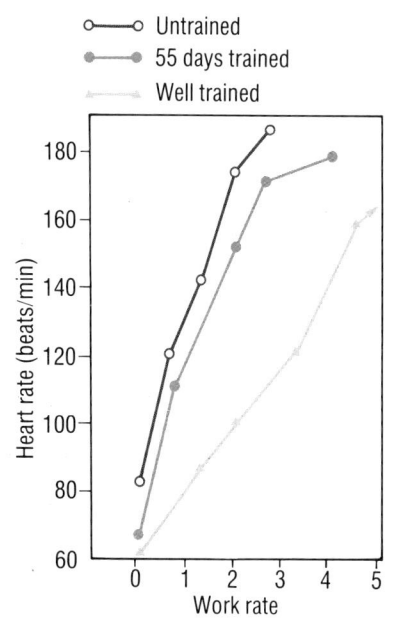

Figure 1. Heart rate at different work rates for three groups of people.

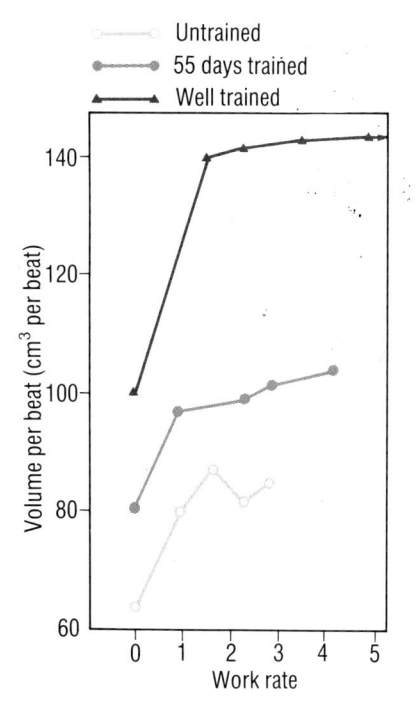

Figure 2. Blood pumped per beat at different work rates.

5.9 Cycle to a stop

All set? I'm on the bike. The heart rate monitor is around my chest, and I've had a few drops of blood taken from one finger. All the bags for my breathed out air are hanging ready on a large frame.

First run. This is easy. The difficult part is pedalling slowly enough! By three minutes and thirty seconds I have fitted the mouthpiece and nose clip so that my breath goes into bag 1 and my rate of breathing is plotted on a chart. Four minutes are up. I sit still for one minute while another blood sample is taken to measure my lactate level.

Away we go again. The bicycle is set at a higher work rate. I could keep this up for hours. The next one is easy too. So it ought to be when I'm only working at the power output of a 100 W light bulb and only for four minutes!

I ask to have the fan put on when the work rate reaches 120 W. I'm getting quite warm. 140 W – OK, but more like hard work! 160 W – this is tougher still, and I'm glad of the one minute rest.

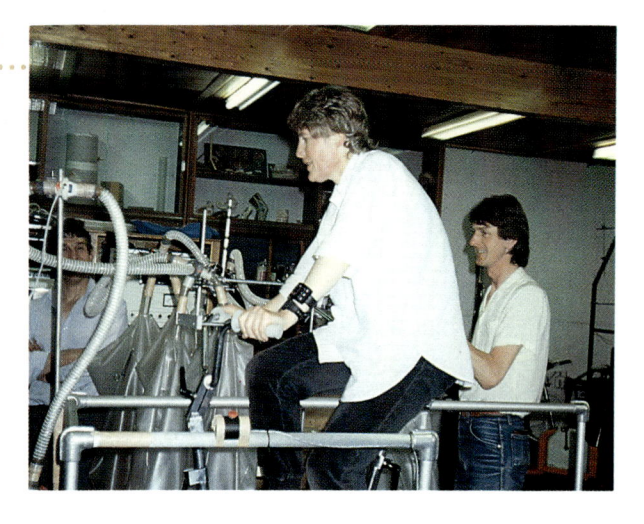

For the last four minutes the work rate goes up to 200 W. This is really hard going. They say my face is red. My blood seems to be hammering in my ears. I'm panting hard. The mouthpiece suddenly seems too difficult to breathe through. Can I go on? Everyone is counting down with me. 20 seconds – you can do it! Only 10 to go! Well done! Now for a rest!

While I pedal gently to recover, the technicians use the equipment to collect all the information. The heart rate monitor is taken off and it prints out my heart rate graph.

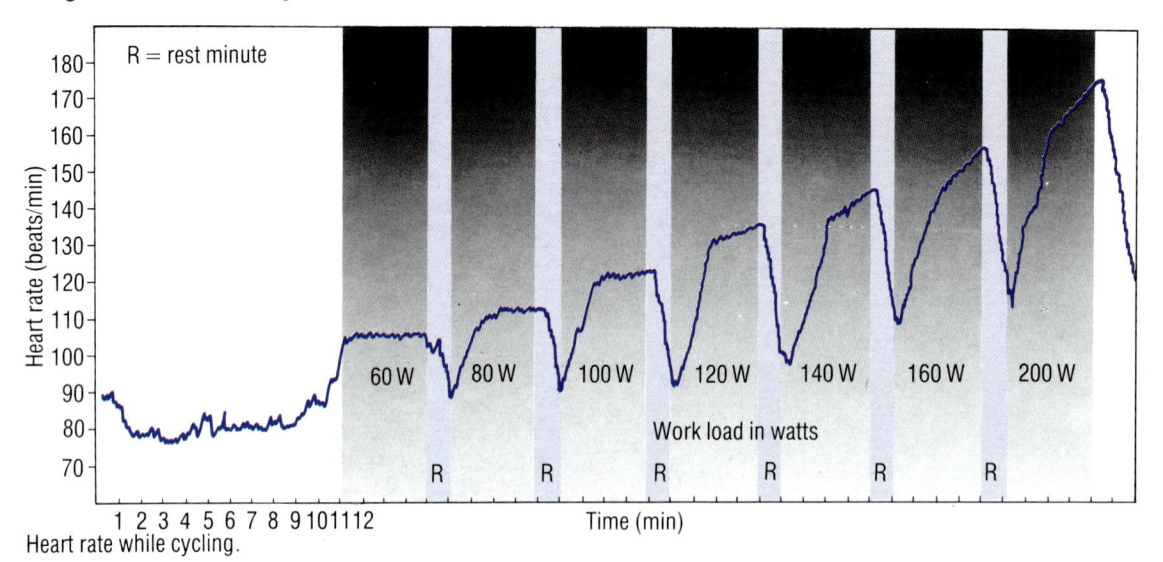

Heart rate while cycling.

When a person starts exercising, their heart rate goes up, but if the body is coping easily the heart rate stops rising and levels out. It is difficult to work really steadily, so the heart rate is not completely even. When the exercise is too hard to be sustained the heart rate during exercise does not level out but continues to rise.

1 What work rates could this cyclist keep up for a long time because her heart can keep up with the demand?

2 What work rates are not possible to sustain and so are leading to exhaustion?

3 Describe what happens to the heart rate during the one-minute rest periods of the experiment.

Heart and lungs together

Changes at different work rates on the exercise bike

Work rate (W)	Heart rate (beats/min)	Breathing rate (breaths/min)	Volume of air expired (litre/min)	Volume of O₂ used (litre/min)	Blood lactate (mg/litre)
0	86	9.6	5.5	0.26	1.0
60	106	10.0	8.0	0.5	1.7
80	112	10.4	8.5	0.7	1.8
100	122	10.4	9.5	0.8	1.5
120	135	11.4	10.5	1.0	3.5
140	143	14.5	12.0	1.3	4.3
160	156	15.8	16.5	1.3	4.5
200	174	30.5	17.5	1.4	9.5

4 Draw line graphs of the results shown above. You can choose to plot each one by itself, or two on one set of axes. Note: each graph needs a different vertical scale.

5 Compare the graphs for breathing and heart rate.
a) Which seems to be affected more at low work rates (up to 120 W)?
b) Which seems to be making the greater changes when the work rate gets higher?

6 Exercise always increases heart rate. If the lungs are damaged they cannot increase the oxygen supply to the blood. What difference would this make to the effect of exercise on heart rate?

7 a) Describe the changes in breathing rate and volume of air expired when changing from 160 W to 200 W work rate.
b) What must have happened to the size of each breath when the person was exhausted and panting?

Training the heart and lungs to meet greater demands

Vigorous exercise strengthens the heart, but for maximum effect the person needs to continue for 20–30 minutes. Too high an exercise level causes lactic acid to build up. Blood lactate levels much above 5 mg/l cause exhaustion so the person stops after only a few minutes.

8 Which work rate made this person's blood lactate go over 5 mg?

9 What does this show about her heart and lungs at this work rate?

10 What work rate would you suggest that she trains at, and why?

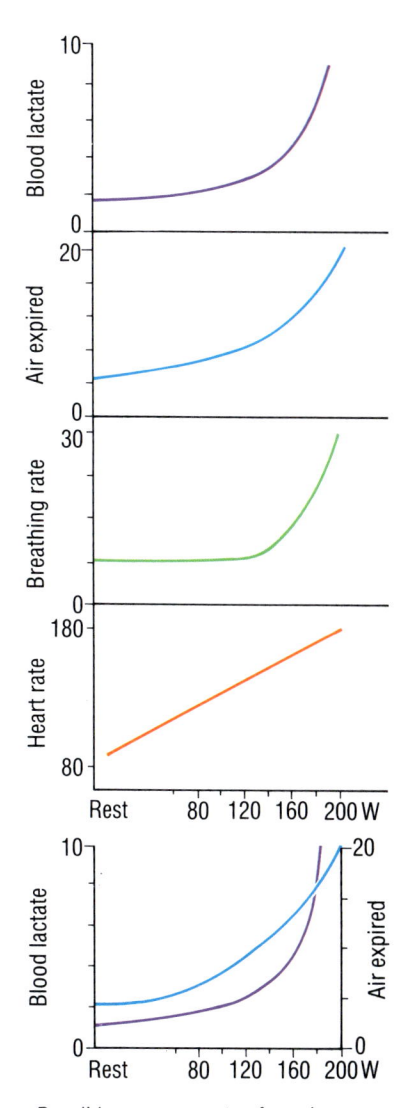

Possible arrangements of graphs.

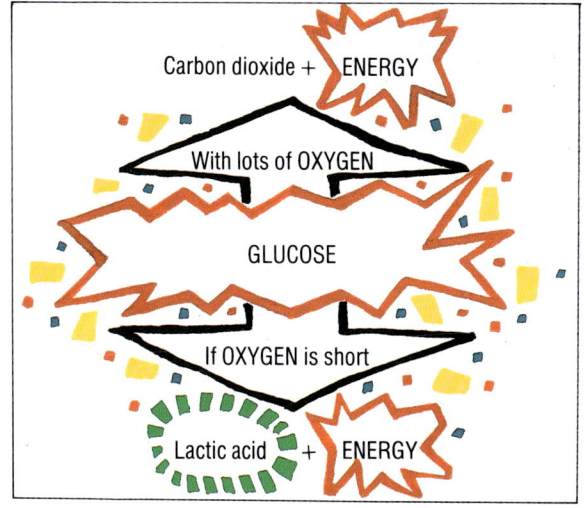

All systems go!

11 How many different systems of the body are in use, and what is each doing, during the last minute of the bike ride?

6.1 What controls the result?

Farmers buy seed that they expect to give a good yield of grain. However, if the spring is very cold, or if there is very little rain during the growing period, the farmers may *not* achieve the crop yields the seed merchants claimed they would.

When you see packets of flower and vegetable seeds in the shops the pictures on them show the *best* plants that you are likely to be able to grow. If you planted the seeds in a dark stony corner of your garden and only weak spindly plants appeared, you could hardly claim a refund from the seedsman. The fault would be yours for putting the seeds in such a poor environment.

We expect the environment to have a marked effect on the development of plants, whatever their genetic background. The same principle applies to humans. For example, a child who has inherited the potential to be a world class athlete may never get a proper chance if she is involved in a bad car accident. Although there can be no mistaking the effects of such an accident, less obvious factors in our environment may influence us in ways which are hard to detect, and even harder to prove.

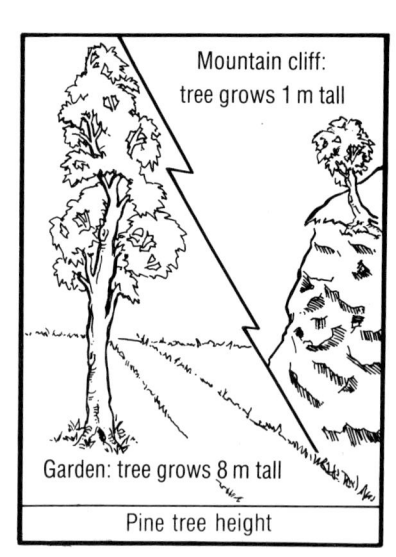

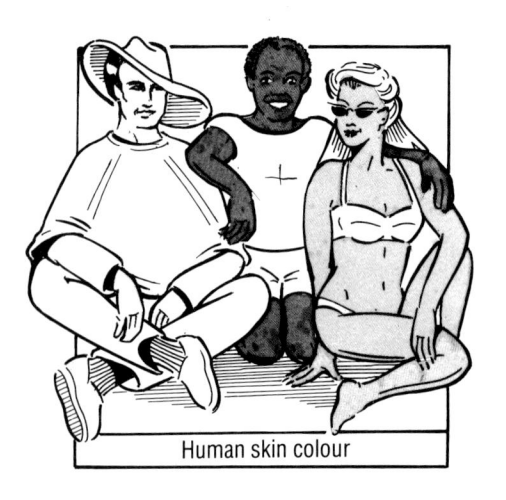

Human skin colour

Milk yield in cattle

Cause of death

Pine tree height
- Mountain cliff: tree grows 1 m tall
- Garden: tree grows 8 m tall

Human eye colour

Cat fur colour

1 The environment may not influence *all* factors. Look at the pictures on this page. Decide whether you think each one is controlled by:
a) genetics alone.
b) environment alone.
c) both together.

Make a table to show your decisions.

The weight of a baby at birth provides one indication of how healthy it is. Small babies are more likely to have health problems than larger ones, although there is a wide range of birth weights that can be considered 'normal'. The average weight of a new born baby is between 3000 g and 3500 g.

The graphs show some results from a study of the birth weights of babies and the levels of certain metals in their mothers' blood. The height of the bar shows the average metal level in the mothers of babies in each weight range.

In the body tissues, these metals are present in very low concentrations. In blood they are measured as micrograms of metal per gram of blood. One microgram (µg) = one thousand thousandth of a gram, or 10^{-6} g.

These results *suggest* that the levels of metals in blood may affect the weight of the baby. The figures are not proof that the metals *cause* the changes in birth weight. Much more research would be needed to be sure of that.

Some campaigners for lead-free petrol argue that lead from car exhausts has been linked to retarded mental development in children. In older housing, children may also be at risk from high levels of lead in the water supply, where pipes are made of lead, instead of copper.

Paints are another source of metal since some contain lead, zinc or cadmium. High levels of zinc are found in some fruit, vegetables and sea fish.

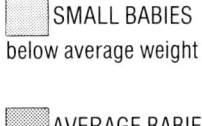

SMALL BABIES
below average weight

AVERAGE BABIES
average birth weight of all babies

HEAVY BABIES
over average birth weight

2 For which *two* of the metals named in the three graphs does increased concentration seem connected with small birth weight of the baby?

3 What seems to be the effect of the concentration of the third metal on birth weight?

4 Poisonous metals are said to be toxic. What do the graphs suggest about which of these metals are toxic?

5 Name at least three factors, other than metal levels, which you think are likely to influence the weight of a baby at birth.

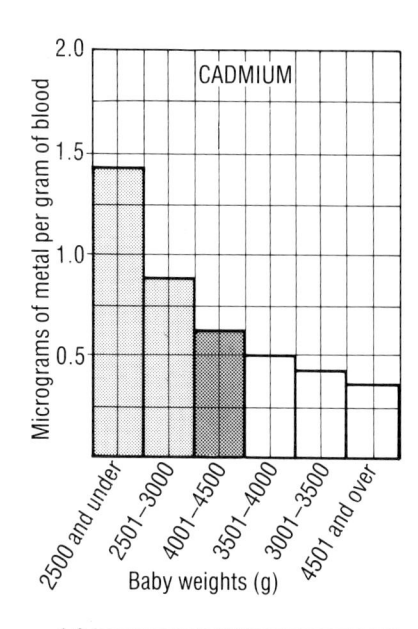

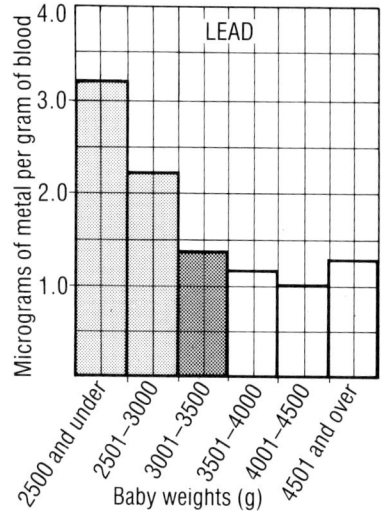

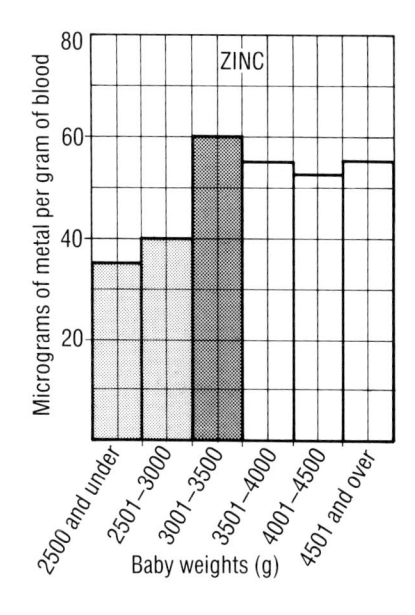

Graphs of metal content of mothers' blood and weights of their babies.

6.2 Family and friends

The sketches on these two pages show nine people in three families. Six of their characteristics are given. These are differences which are inherited, assuming that none of the individuals have dyed their hair.

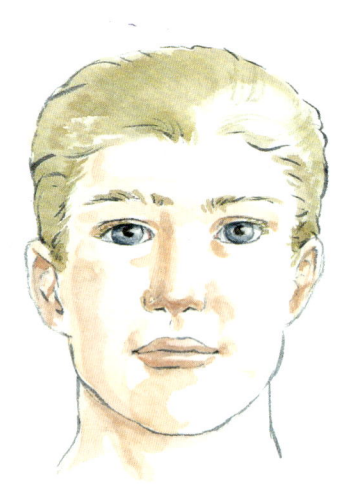

EDDIE BROWN
blond hair
peak
dark eyes
no lobes
no gap
roller

CHRIS COLLINS
red hair
no peak
blue eyes
lobes
gap
roller

HUGH COLLINS
brown hair
no peak
green eyes
lobes
gap
roller

GILL COLLINS
brown hair
no peak
blue eyes
lobes
no gap
roller

1 Do you expect people to be more like their families or more like their friends? Why?

2 a) Make a table to show the characteristics of the nine people.
b) Is anyone identical to anyone else?

The next questions allow you to give each person a score which shows whether the people in the pictures are more like their families or their friends.

3 Make a table, like Table 1, for the results of your calculations. Start with Alan. Read how his score was calculated, and put it in your table.

Table 1

Name	Family score	Friends score
Alan		

Family scores

4 Alan's family are the other Abbots, Fred and Iris. Alan and Fred are alike in five ways. Score 5. Alan and Iris are also alike in five ways. Again score 5.
So Alan's family score is

$$\frac{5+5}{2} = \frac{10}{2} = 5.$$

a) Choose one of the Browns. Write the name in your table. Calculate the family score for that person and record it.
b) Choose one of the Collins family. Write the name in your table. Calculate the family score for that person and record it.

ALAN ABBOT
dark hair
no peak
dark eyes
lobes
no gap
not roller

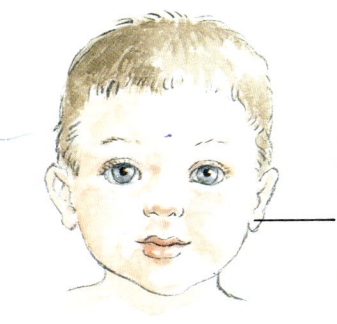

FRED ABBOT
dark hair
no peak
green eyes
lobes
no gap
not roller

IRIS ABBOT
dark hair
peak
dark eyes
lobes
no gap
not roller

Friends scores

5 For this task people are 'friends' with the people of the same sex in the other families. For example, Alan's friends are the two other boys, Eddie and Hugh.
Alan and Eddie are alike in two characteristics. Alan and Hugh are also alike in two ways.
So Alan's friends score is

$$\frac{2+2}{2} = \frac{4}{2} = 2.$$

If you choose someone who needs to be compared with three people, to get their score add the three 'alike' totals and divide by three. That is:

$$\text{score} = \frac{\text{total number of similarities with other people}}{\text{the number of other people}}$$

Calculate the friends scores for the people that you have already chosen, and record your answers.

BETTY BROWN
blonde hair
no peak
blue eyes
no lobes
no gap
roller

peak

DAWN BROWN
blonde hair
peak
blue eyes
no lobes
no gap
roller

6 Does your table show what you expected it to?

7 In what way is this method of scoring differences better than saying, 'Of course people look more like their families'?

8 You could try calculating your own 'family score' and comparing it with your own 'friends score'.

6.3 Robert the footballer

'When I grow up I want to be a footballer!' cried Robert to his Dad. But Robert is not like other healthy boys of six. He is being pushed in his wheelchair to the hospital for another check-up. The disease he is suffering from affects all the muscles of the body, gradually making them weak as they turn from healthy muscle to fatty tissue.

Robert has a disease called **Duchenne muscular dystrophy**, but he has not *caught* the disease in the usual way we become ill, through catching a bug. He has inherited it from his parents, or to be more exact, from his mother.

Although Robert's mother does not herself suffer from the disease, the gene for it is on one of the chromosomes in each of her body's cells. Her egg, which was fertilized to produce Robert, had that gene in it right from the start. Robert's sister, Lisa, may also have inherited the gene from their mother. The strange thing is that even if she has, she will never show any symptoms of the disease. She may, however, pass it on to her son. Every time a mother carrying the gene has a son, he has a 50% chance of inheriting the disease.

1 Duchenne muscular dystrophy is a hereditary condition. What does this mean?

2 How did Robert get the disease?

3 If Lisa is a carrier, what are the chances of her son inheriting the disease from her?

When Robert was a baby, he seemed very slow in learning to walk, preferring to shuffle on his behind. The health visitor said at that stage that there was nothing to worry about; plenty of children were lazy about talking or walking and otherwise he seemed quite normal. He seemed to cope quite well for the first year at school. Then his teacher noticed that he was less active than other children and seemed to tire more easily. A check-up at the hospital showed that all was not well. Robert had muscular dystrophy, which will probably cause heart or breathing failure when he is still a young man.

In the meantime, some help can be provided to make him more comfortable. A local muscular dystrophy group has provided him with a 'wellie boot machine', which helps the blood circulation in his legs. They also run trips to the seaside, the zoo and other places. These not only help Robert but also allow his Mum and Dad to have a break from the strain of giving him the constant care and attention he needs.

Although a lot of work will have to be done before a treatment or a cure are found, doctors are developing a more efficient technique for detecting women who carry the disease. They can then offer advice to couples who may be likely to have a baby with muscular dystrophy.

4 How does the condition affect Robert?

5 What can be done to help him at present?

6 In what two ways are doctors tackling the problem of Duchenne muscular dystrophy?

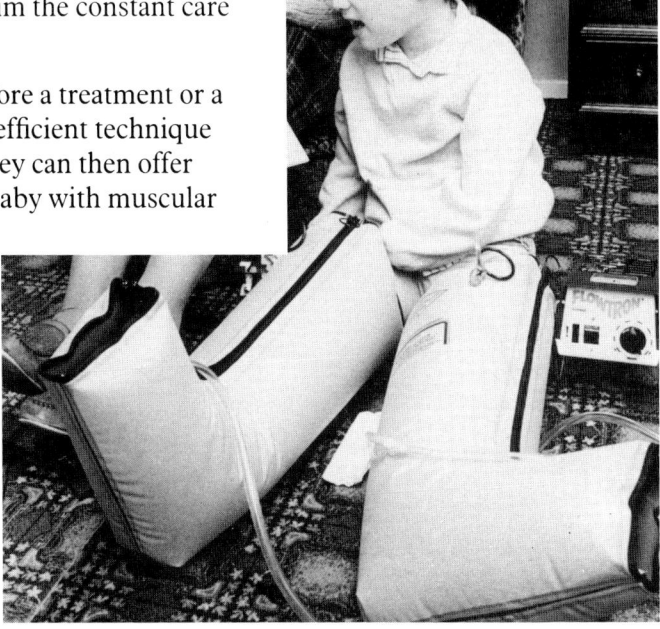

Diseases which are inherited in the same way as muscular dystrophy are called **sex-linked** because the chance of a person getting them depends on whether the person is male or female. The harmful gene is recessive, and is on one of the X chromosomes in Robert's mother's cells.

7 Draw diagrams including X and Y symbols to show the sex-chromosomes and disease gene in:
a) one of Robert's mother's cells and the types of eggs that she can produce.
b) one of Robert's father's cells and the types of sperm he can produce.
c) the fertilized egg which became Robert.
d) the fertilized egg that became Lisa, assuming she is a carrier.

8 Assume Lisa is a carrier. Explain why her sons have a 50% chance of having muscular dystrophy and why none of her daughters could have it.

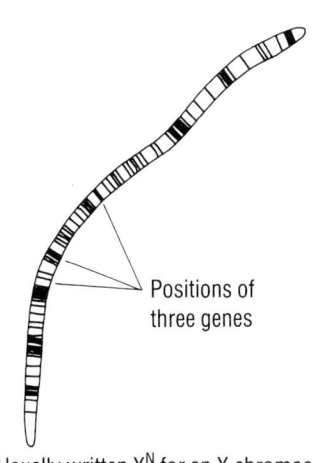

Usually written X^N for an X chromosome with normal genes or X^{MD} for one carrying a muscular dystrophy gene.

An X chromosome.

6.4 Lucky Stephanie

Carlos and Maria have a healthy two-year-old girl. Since both have a family history of a serious blood disease called **thalassaemia** they are lucky to have a healthy child at all.

When they first decided to have a baby, Carlos and Maria both went for a blood test. They found that they were both carriers of thalassaemia. Although they were both perfectly healthy and did not suffer in any way from the disease, they might well pass it on to any child they had.

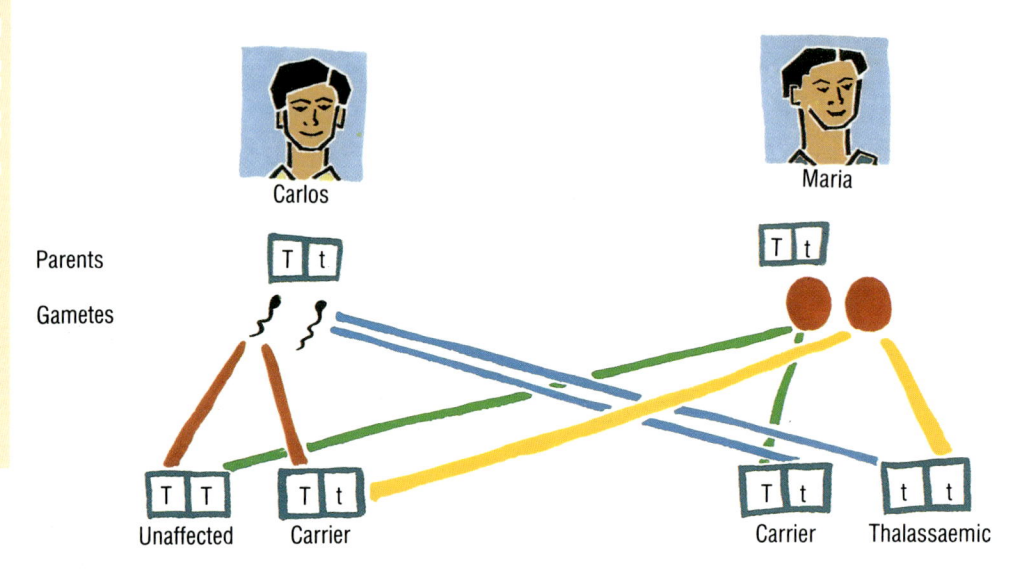

Pattern of inheritance of thalassaemia gene.

They arranged to meet a genetic counsellor to discuss this worrying situation. She told them that children affected by thalassaemia are often born normal but start to show symptoms of the disease at about 6–9 months. These children are anaemic. They cannot make their own blood cells and have to depend for the rest of their lives on 'borrowed blood', which they get by transfusion.

How can children get the disease from healthy parents? The answer lies in the genes passed on from one generation to the next. The thalassaemia gene is **recessive** and may be hidden by its normal partner-gene or allele on the chromosomes. The normal gene is therefore said to be **dominant**. For both Carlos and Maria this was the explanation. Both parents had one gene for thalassaemia. Both also had one normal gene that concealed their gene for thalassaemia.

1 What would first suggest to a couple that they could be carriers of thalassaemia even though they are both perfectly healthy?

2 It is possible at present to test reliably for 'carriers' of only some genetic diseases. What are the advantages of such a test?

3 When would it be best to have a blood test if you suspect you may be a carrier for a genetic disease? Explain your answer.

4 Carlos and Maria were both carriers for thalassaemia. Their daughter Stephanie was completely normal. Explain how to calculate the chances of this happening.

5 What are the chances that their next child would be:
a) completely normal?
b) a carrier?
c) thalassaemic?

Doctors have developed a blood test for 'carriers' of thalassaemia. This was the blood test that Carlos and Maria had, which showed that they each had one normal gene and one thalassaemia gene. Unfortunately the blood tests can only give an estimate of the *chances* of having an affected child. To find whether the child is actually affected we need to do further tests during the pregnancy.

When Maria was 18 weeks pregnant she went into hospital so that the baby could be tested. Using an ultrasound scan to check the position of the baby, the doctor slid a needle carefully through Maria's abdomen and into her womb. She drew out a small sample of fluid and embryo cells from the water sac around the baby. This technique is called **amniocentesis**.

A pregnant woman having a scan.

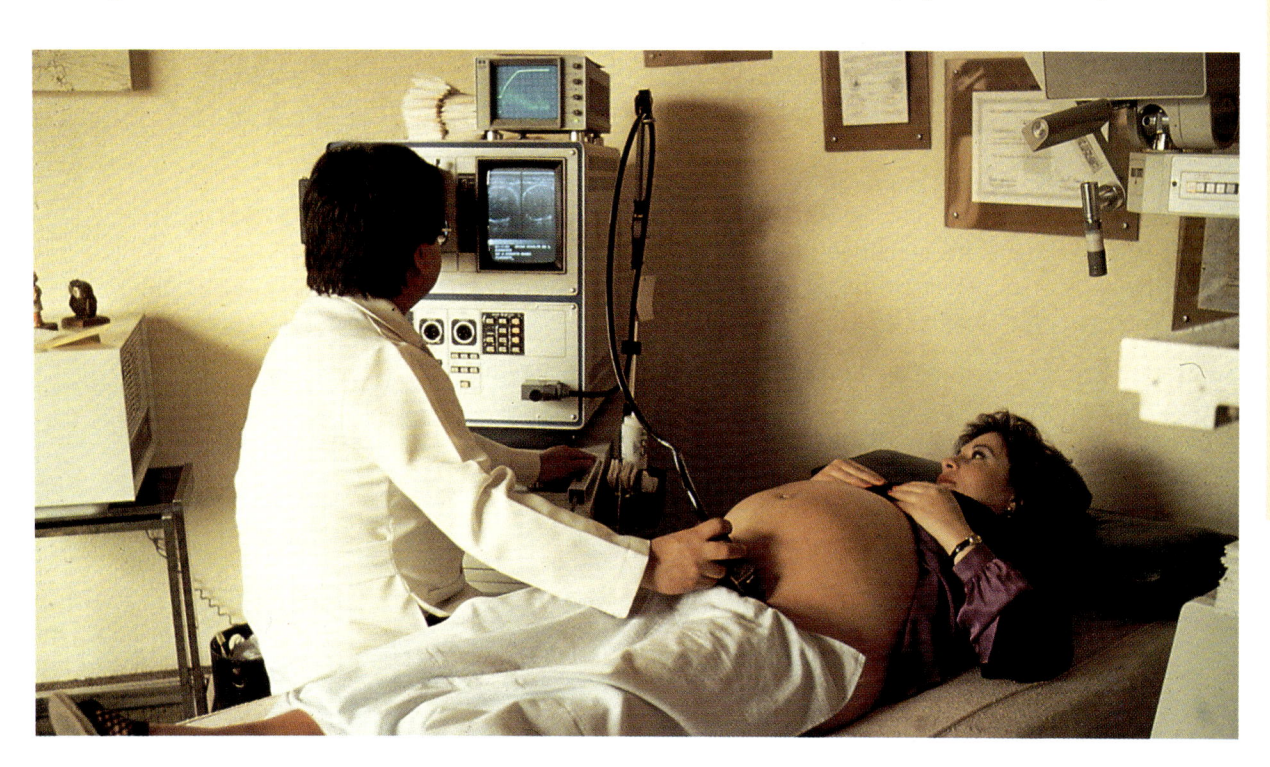

The cells were specially treated so that the chromosomes showed up. The genes on the chromosomes of these cells were examined for abnormalities. The result was all that Carlos and Maria had hoped for. Seven months later their beautiful daughter Stephanie was born. She was completely free from thalassaemia, not even a carrier like her parents.

6 What difficult decision would Maria and Carlos have had to make if the amniocentesis had shown the child to have thalassaemia?

7 The blood test showed that both Carlos and Maria were carriers of thalassaemia. If no test had been possible on the baby, how do you think this would influence their decision to try for a baby?

8 Find out about and make a list of other genetic diseases that are inherited as a recessive gene from the parents.

6.5 Will baby be all right?

Some couples planning to have children may know that there is inherited disease in their family. A genetic counsellor can advise them of the chances that faulty genes in their chromosomes might appear in their sex cells and be passed on to harm their child.

Even those with no history of inherited disease may be concerned about possible embryo abnormalities. The risk of having a child with chromosome abnormalities increases with the age of the mother. Mothers over the age of 35 are usually advised to be screened.

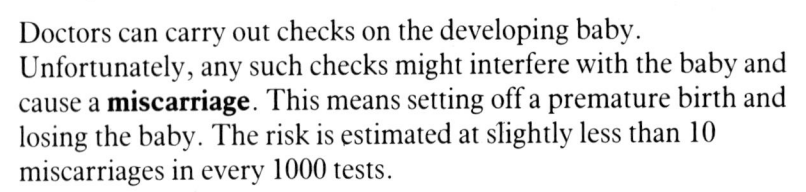

Doctors can carry out checks on the developing baby. Unfortunately, any such checks might interfere with the baby and cause a **miscarriage**. This means setting off a premature birth and losing the baby. The risk is estimated at slightly less than 10 miscarriages in every 1000 tests.

Some abnormalities in unborn children can be detected by looking at the chromosomes of cells which came from the same fertilized egg cell as the foetus. The two methods most used are amniocentesis and the newer technique of chorionic villus sampling (CVS). CVS seems to have several advantages, but a research programme is needed to make sure that there are no unexpected risks.

Risk of chromosome abnormality with age of mother

Age of mother	Abnormalities per 1000 births
25	1
35	3
40	10
45	25

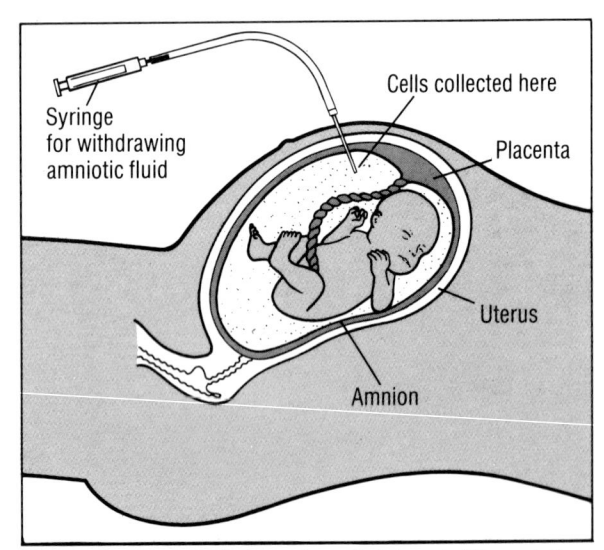

The amniocentesis technique. A needle is inserted through the abdomen and cells are removed for study.

Amniocentesis

An ultrasound scan is used to find the position of the baby and the placenta. After a local anaesthetic, a needle is inserted through the mother's abdomen until it reaches the water sac around the baby. Some of the fluid is drawn off and the baby is again checked with ultrasound. The cells in the fluid are then grown for two weeks and their chromosomes are checked for abnormalities.

A disadvantage of amniocentesis is that it cannot be carried out until the sixteenth week of pregnancy. The results are not known for about another two weeks so the pregnancy is well advanced before the couple know if the baby is normal.

Chorionic villus sampling

In chorionic villus sampling a fine tube is slid through the vagina to take a sample of villus cells. The villi are projections of tissue at the placenta, and have the same chromosomes as the foetus.

CVS has the advantage that it can be carried out at 8–12 weeks. The cells can also be examined at once, without needing to be grown for two weeks.

Normal

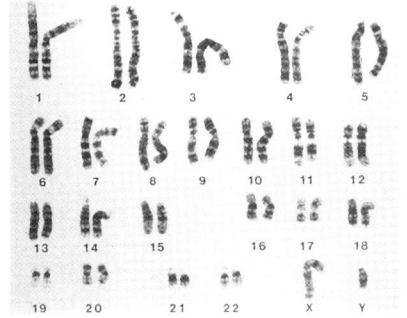

Down's Syndrome

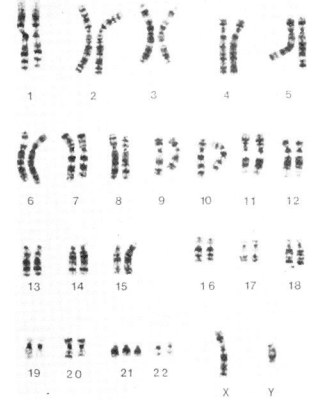

Chorionic villus sampling. A fine tube is inserted through the vagina and cells are removed for study.

Each of these two sets of chromosomes comes from a single cell obtained by amniocentesis. Can you see a difference in the number of chromosomes in each set? The extra chromosome in one set causes Down's syndrome – an inherited disease.

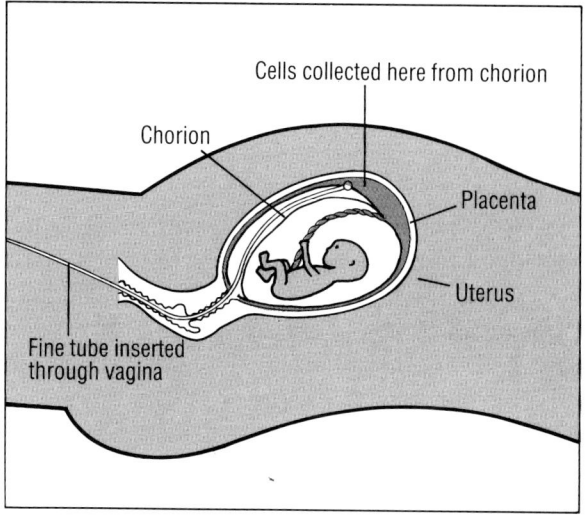

Difficult decisions

If an abnormality is detected by either method the parents are faced with a difficult decision. They have to decide whether or not to end the pregnancy.

If the couple decide to keep the pregnancy knowing that the baby will have problems, they will need a great deal of help and support.

The couple may decide to end the pregnancy. Even though they feel that this is the better decision, they may suffer a dreadful sense of grief over the lost child.

If a woman has to have a termination, she will need a lot of love and understanding from her partner and from those around her after such a sad experience. Some such women find it helpful to have professional counselling or to join a women's support group, where they can discuss their shared problem. The sense of grief will be greater the longer the pregnancy has gone on.

1 From the information given, which has the higher probability for a 35-year-old pregnant woman: miscarriage brought on by amniocentesis or giving birth to a child with a chromosome abnormality?

2 Compare the techniques of amniocentesis and chorionic villus sampling by answering these questions.
a) Which can be carried out earlier and why is this an advantage?
b) Which gives the quickest diagnosis? Explain why.

3 A couple are told that an unborn child is affected by a genetic disease. What difficulties might the couple face:
a) if the pregnancy is terminated?
b) if the pregnancy is allowed to go to full term?

4 In what three ways might a woman get support after a termination?

5 Study Figure 1 carefully. What is different about the Down's syndrome chromosome set?

6.6 Improving plants

Almost all the plants that people grow have been specially bred to improve yield and quality. Breeders want roses with large flowers or peaches which keep well, for example. All these plants have wild ancestors, although we might find them hard to recognize. For example, wheat is descended from a wild grass which had rather small seeds and too long a stalk. Early farmers kept aside the seed from the plants with the largest grains and shortest stems to be sown in the following year. When this selection of the best is continued for many years, eventually the new 'biggest' variety of plant is much larger than any that were in the original wild population. Because the growth of plants is controlled by several genes working together, this selection process may take several crosses to bring the best genes into one plant.

Other crops we take for granted are potatoes and tomatoes. Both grow wild in South America but they are so small, and the potatoes are such odd colours, that it is hard to believe they are varieties of the ones we buy from the supermarket. However, these new, attractive and profitable plants may have some disadvantages. They may easily become diseased or only grow well when given a lot of fertilizer.

This is where wild plants still have their uses. Some of the wild varieties may be more resistant to diseases, for example, or may have a stronger root system than our cultivated varieties. The plant breeder can use wild plants to introduce these features into his commercial stocks and improve them by special breeding programmes.

When a plant reproduces normally an insect or the wind carries the pollen to the stigma. This means that chance decides which pollen fertilizes an egg cell. A plant breeder needs to be able to choose the parents of the crosses she makes. To do this she must control pollination. Sometimes this is done by using a paintbrush to carry the pollen from one variety of flower to the stigma of another variety. This can be very slow and painstaking work. The aim is to produce seeds which carry the best features of both parents.

The variety of daffodils available is large – and growing.

Same species – different varieties!

Cross-pollination

Breeding programme for improving tomatoes.

Plant A₁: Wild plant, fruit all poisonous, strong roots

Plant A₂: Cultivated plant, good fruit but few because of very poor roots

Plant B₁: A few good fruit, poor roots
Plant B₂: A few good fruit, strong roots
Plant B₃: Very few good fruit, poor roots
Plant B₄: A few good fruit, fair roots
Plant B₅: A few good fruit, strong roots

Plant C₁: More good fruit, strong roots
Plant C₂: More good fruit, poor roots
Plant C₃: A few good fruit, fair roots
Plant C₄: More good fruit, strong roots
Plant C₅: Some good fruit, poor roots

Best of these improved plants used to continue another five generations of crosses to produce:

Plant H: Only good fruit, because of strong roots

The diagram above shows a breeding programme. The aim is to produce tomato plants with good, large fruit and a strong root system. The two parent plants are A_1 and A_2. The first generation (B plants) is quite varied.

1 Describe the two parent plants.

2 Which two B plants are shown as being crossed to produce the C plants? Why were these two chosen?

3 Which two C plants would you use for the next cross?

4 Describe the result of this breeding programme.

5 Biologists are concerned about the disappearance of many wild varieties of plants. Explain how wild varieties of plant might be of importance to plant breeders.

6 In the diagram, many crosses are necessary to breed the new plant. Suggest some reasons why the results cannot be produced with just one cross.

7 If plant H tended to suffer from disease, explain how you would set up a breeding programme to introduce disease resistance.

6.7 Mutations

Why do cats' fertilized eggs develop into kittens and not into puppies? How do your muscle cells 'know' that they have to contract rather than produce saliva?

Every cell, including egg-cells, is controlled by the chromosomes in its nucleus. **DNA**, which makes up part of each chromosome, carries the coded information needed to control the cell. Any change in this information will make the cell behave differently.

These changes in DNA are called **mutations** and are normally very rare. A mutation in a fertilized egg cell may cause it to develop wrongly or not at all. A mutation in a body cell might make it start to divide uncontrollably, causing a cancer.

His skin colour doesn't match his parents'. Think what problems this might cause.

It is quite common to find offspring with some features not shown by either parent. They may have inherited these from their grandparents. However, *mutations* in sperms or eggs can produce offspring that show totally new features which did not exist in *any* of their earlier ancestors.

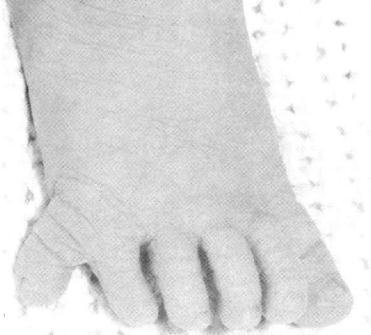

Some mutations are caused by mistakes in copying DNA during cell division. Others result from direct damage to DNA by chemicals or radiation.

None of this person's family ever had feet like this!

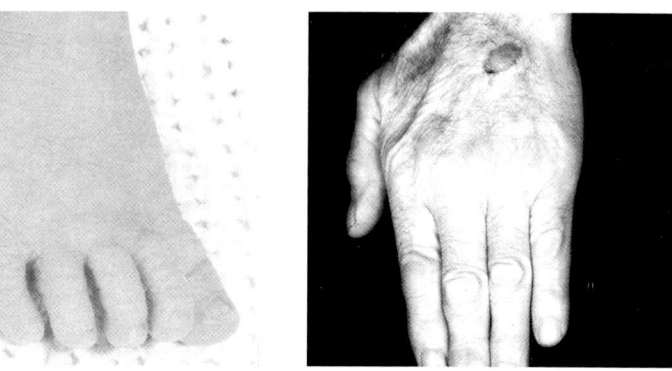

This cancer was caused by over-exposure to ultra-violet light.

The pie chart shows the different sources of radiation to which we are exposed today. Our total lifetime dose is estimated to cause only one mutation per 50 000 people.

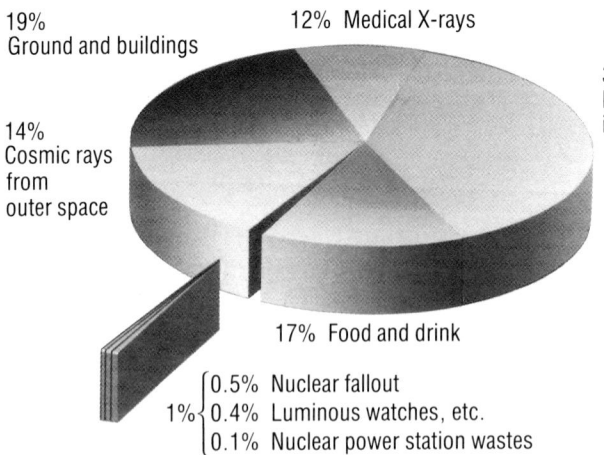

- 19% Ground and buildings
- 12% Medical X-rays
- 37% Natural radioactivity in air
- 14% Cosmic rays from outer space
- 17% Food and drink
- 1% { 0.5% Nuclear fallout / 0.4% Luminous watches, etc. / 0.1% Nuclear power station wastes }

Where the radiation comes from.

1 What are mutations?

2 What causes mutations?

3 Name two kinds of change that mutations can cause.

4 a) What percentage of our radiation dose is natural 'background radiation', to which living things have always been exposed?
b) What percentage is man-made and therefore new?

5 Skin cancer is commoner in people who have emigrated from Britain to Australia than it is in their relatives at home. Explain why this might happen.

Mutations have been of great value in helping us understand how inheritance works. Unfortunately for the scientists, they are very rare. Many biologists have tried to find ways of producing more mutations to study. In some early experiments animals were exposed to X-rays to produce the mutations. Ultra-violet light (like in bright sunshine) and certain chemicals like mustard gas were also found to produce the changes in DNA which cause mutations.

We now know of many more mutation-causing chemicals, or **mutagens**. The tar from cigarette smoke is one of the best known, but many chemicals used in industry have similar effects.

A *Drosophila* fly with abnormal wings as a result of radiation.

Figure 1 shows the rates of mutation produced by exposing *Drosophila* fruit flies to different doses of X-rays.

Note that the graph does *not* show the percentage of mutations produced at radiation doses lower than 500 mSv. This is because so few mutations are produced at these radiation levels that we would need to study huge numbers of flies to find even a few mutants.

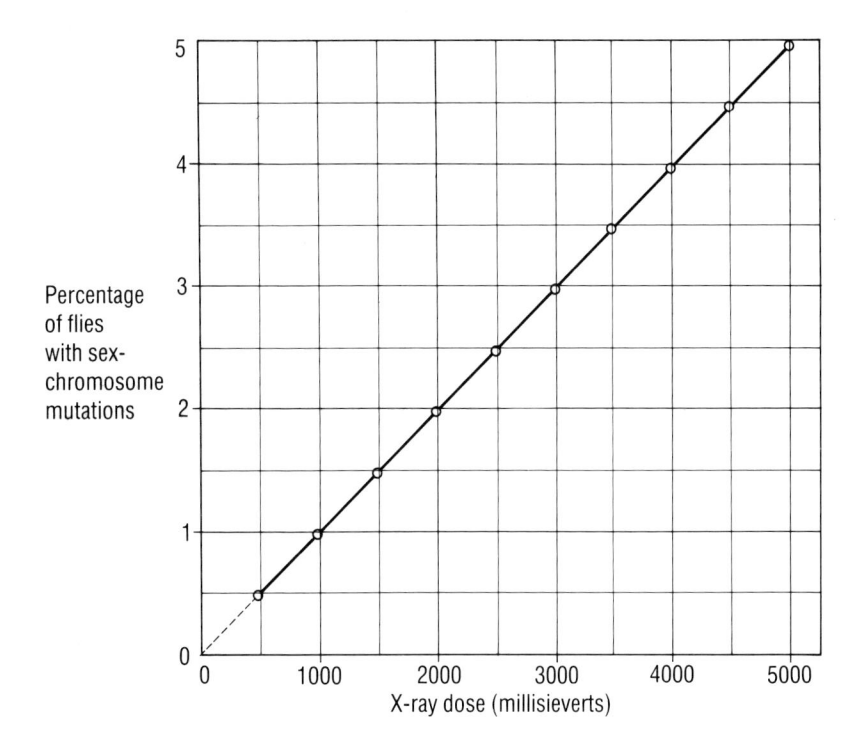

Figure 1. Percentage of *Drosophila* flies with mutated sex-chromosomes, at different doses of radiation.

6 According to the graph, what is the relationship between radiation dose and the number of mutations produced?

7 What would the graph predict to be the number of mutations produced by a radiation dose of zero?

8 a) In a control experiment, flies were given no X-rays. About 0.25% of these untreated flies showed mutations. What level of 'background radiation' from their surroundings would be needed to produce this proportion of mutants?
b) *Drosophila* flies only live for four weeks. The total dose a fly could accumulate from background radiation in this time is only 0.15mSv. What does this suggest about the cause of mutations in *Drosophila* flies?

7.1 Uses of microbes

Figure 1. Spot which of these are made using microbes.

'Microbes', that is bacteria and fungi, have been used by people since ancient times. Possibly the effects of alcohol were first noticed by Stone Age people after eating old honey or over-ripe fruit. The main developments since then have been in the control of the process.

'**Old biotechnology**' is ancient. The products are foods and drinks. The processes are, or were, very simple. For example, yogurt can be made by adding lactic acid bacteria to warm milk in a container. The simplest form of cheese making just involves mixing a bacterial 'starter' with milk and leaving it to turn acid and coagulate. Of course, to make food everything needs to be clean, but sterile techniques are not necessary. Certainly, more reliable products are made if cleaner and better controlled conditions are used, and modern biotechnology 'factories', such as breweries, do steam sterilize their huge containers and equipment.

Yeast is one of the most useful microbes. The carbon dioxide it produces makes bread rise. It can feed on and ferment sugar solutions to produce alcohol. Fermentation *originally* just meant alcohol production by yeast, but any product whose label mentions fermentation has been made with the help of microbes.

World markets for ten products of biotechnology

Figures for early 1980s, in millions of dollars			
Top six			**Key**
*	Alcoholic drinks	34 000	* Food and
*	Cheese	21 000	drinks
µ#	Antibiotics	6750	µ Medicine
€	Fuel alcohol	4000	€ Energy
µ	Diagnostic tests for diseases	3000	# Agriculture
*	Sugar syrups	1200	
Some others from the top twenty in a league table of products			
µ	Steroid drugs	650	
*	MSG flavour enhancer	550	
µ	Vaccines	225	
#	Microbial insecticides	18	

1 Which of the products shown in Figure 1 have been made using microbes?

2 Write a short paragraph to describe what the table suggests about biotechnology in different industries. Compare the size of the market for 'food and drink' biotechnology with the biotechnology market in other industries.

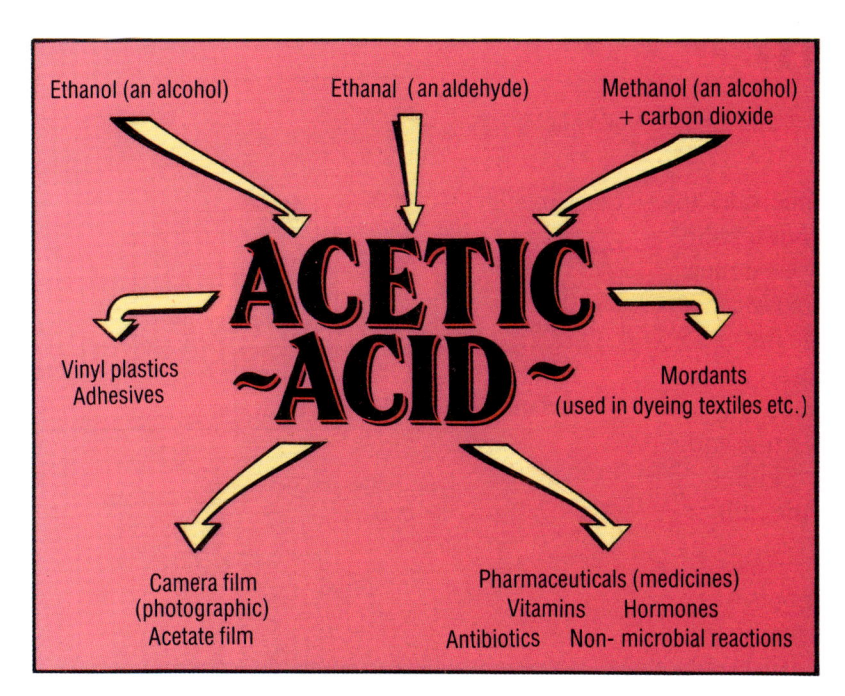

Microbes can make acetic acid from several substances. It is then used to make other products.

Some people want non-fattening sweeteners. This one is made by microbes.

BIOTECHNOLOGY

'**New biotechnology**' has developed since about 1950. The processes are always carried out in sterile conditions. Variables like temperature and aeration of the growing medium must be precisely controlled.

It is hard to appreciate just how important biotechnology is. Many products of biotechnology are used to produce something else. For example, animals raised for meat may have been fed a growth promoter made by microbes. Products made by biotechnology are used in exactly the same way as if they came from another source. The labels on everyday items do not normally show whether microbes were used in their production. Ethanoic acid used in making adhesives may have been produced by biotechnology or by some other chemical process.

The table shows four areas where biotechnology is important. The chemical industry also uses products made by microbes. It may use more if oil prices rise, so that biotechnology becomes the cheaper source. Microbes can also be used to prevent and clean up pollution.

Every month fresh possibilities for the uses of biotechnology, although not always microbes, are announced in the newspapers. However, only some of these will work out well.

3 The text and diagrams on these two pages say something about the uses of biotechnology. Make your own notes on this information. You may want to put it in a table like the one below, or in a 'spider' diagram. You may prefer a different way of summarizing information.

These two pages have *not* mentioned everything; you may want to add other examples of the uses of biotechnology to your notes as you find out about them.

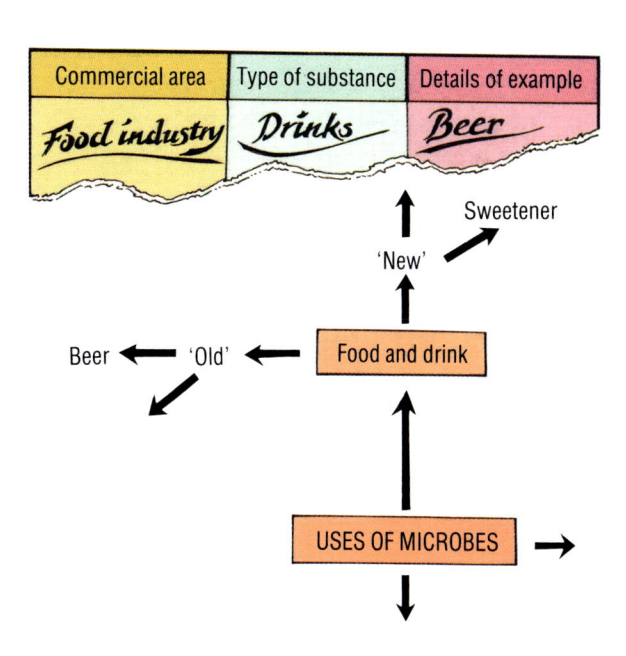

Commercial area	Type of substance	Details of example
Food industry	Drinks	Beer

7.2 Cell growth

BIOTECHNOLOGY

Biotechnology often depends on tiny microbes to produce useful chemicals, like ethanol or insulin. If genetically engineered microbes are used then the starting point may be *one single bacterium* carrying the correct gene. How can one tiny microbe produce anything useful? The secret is in its rate of growth and multiplication. Under ideal conditions each bacterial cell can grow and divide into two new cells every 20–30 minutes. The total number doubles every time the cells divide.

1 Copy out the table of times and numbers in Figure 1 and complete it to show how many bacterial cells there would be at every half-hour up to four hours after the start.

2 Draw a line graph to show the rate of growth.

3 Work out how many cells there would be eight hours after the start.

As you can see, the numbers quickly become enormous! At this rate of increase one bacterium would produce millions of tonnes of offspring in as little as two days! This explains how a single genetically engineered bacterium can be made to supply large quantities of product. Each cell produces only tiny amounts, but the millions of cells together produce a worthwhile quantity.

Counting microbes by direct counting

How do we count these huge numbers of microbes? **Direct counting** is the simplest way. We take a tiny drop of the liquid they are growing in, and look at it under a microscope.

Sometimes the numbers are so large that we need to dilute the original liquid 100 or 1000 times to have a small enough number to count on our slide. This method counts every cell, but does not show whether each cell is alive or dead.

Cell Growth

Time after start (hours)	0	½	1	1½	2	2½	3	3½	4
Total number	1	2	4	8					

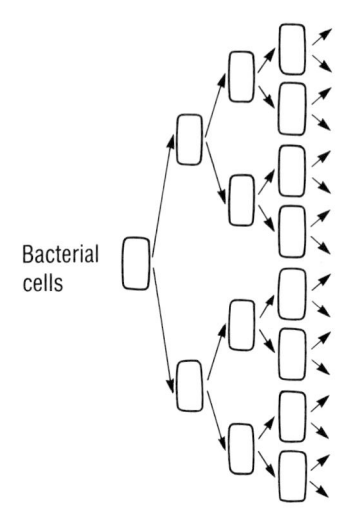

Figure 1. The number of bacteria produced if each one divides every half-hour.

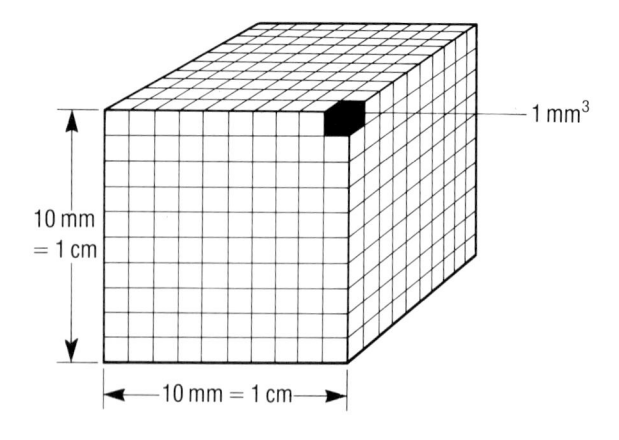

$1 cm^3 = 1000 mm^3$

So 100 cells in $1 mm^3$ = 100 000 cells in $1 cm^3$

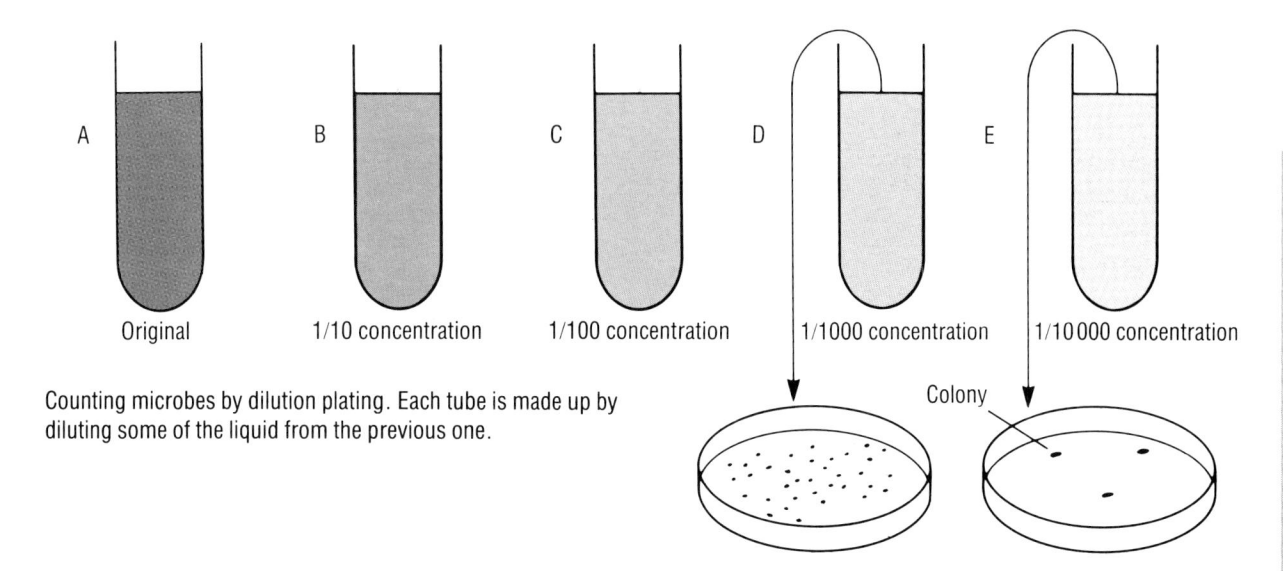

Counting microbes by dilution plating. Each tube is made up by diluting some of the liquid from the previous one.

Counting microbes by dilution plating

Dilution plating is another way of counting. We make up a series of tubes, with the original liquid diluted as shown above.

We take a 1 cm³ sample from each of the last few tubes and pour it with nutrient agar on a plate. Each single cell grows and divides to produce a 'colony' that we can easily see with the naked eye. Thirty colonies on plate D means 30 bacterial cells per cm³ in tube D. This means that there must have been 30 000 per cm³ in the original solution A. This method depends on the cells being active and able to grow to produce the colony.

In practice, the number of cells does *not* keep doubling for ever. Food supplies run out and poisonous waste products build up.

Look at direct count A in Table 1.

4 Describe clearly the changes in cell numbers from the start until 36 hours.

5 When do the cell numbers seem to be increasing fastest?

6 What must be happening, that explains the cell numbers between 12 and 36 hours?

Look at dilution plating count B in Table 1.

7 In general, how do the numbers differ from the total cell count in A?

Table 1. Direct and dilution counts of bacteria growing in a flask of nutrient broth

Hours	Total no. of cells/cm³ A (Direct count)	No. of cells/cm³ B (dilution plating)
0	20 000	20 000
2	27 200	21 900
4	540 000	496 000
6	6 400 000	5 430 000
8	105 760 000	81 900 000
12	126 300 000	83 400 000
24	127 600 000	80 500 000
36	127 900 000	1 120 000

8 What does this mean about some of the cells counted in A?

9 What seems to happen from 24 to 36 hours?

10 Suggest reasons why this might happen.

11 Which counting method, A or B, would be more useful for predicting the likely amount of product from genetically engineered microbes, and why?

7.3 The sewage works filter bed

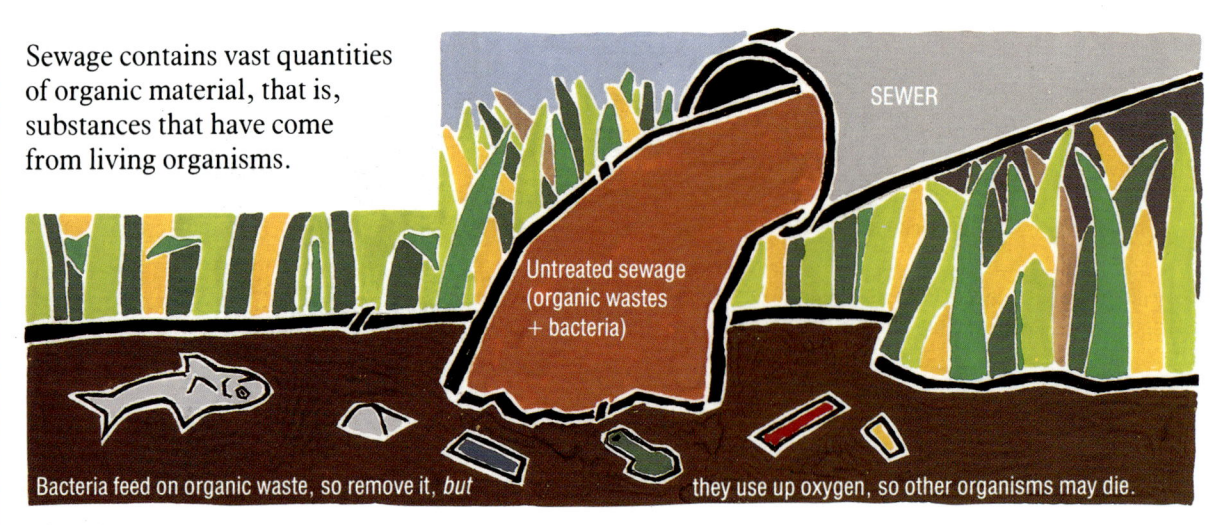

Sewage contains vast quantities of organic material, that is, substances that have come from living organisms.

Effect of untreated sewage on a river.

The task of the sewage works is to remove the organic material before the water is discharged into the river. This is done in two main stages. Most of the organic solids are settled out as 'sludge', which is treated separately. The remaining liquid is treated by *bacteria* in the filter bed system.

The bacteria work best with lots of oxygen. The thin films in the filter bed give them plenty of oxygen from the air between the stones (Figure 1). Other organisms also live in the film (Figure 2). They feed on the bacteria and stop the film getting too thick.

When water in the sewage works is analysed, four measurements are usually made, as shown in Table 1.

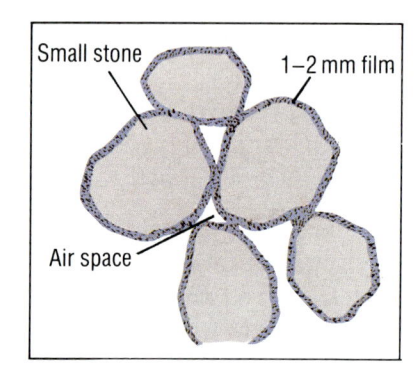

Figure 1. Watery film (1–2 mm thick) on the stones contains bacteria and other organisms.

Table 1. Measurements at different stages in the sewage works. These figures could be from the sewage works of any country town, and are averaged over a year

	SS (mg/l)	BOD (mg/l)	Compounds of nitrogen	
			Ammonia (mg/l)	Nitrate (mg/l)
Crude sewage	250	180	20–30	0
After primary settlement	100	100	18–25	0
After trickle filter bed (and resettlement to remove bacteria)	25	19	9	10

SS stands for **suspended solids** and means small solid particles, mainly of organic material but including some minerals, in the water.

BOD stands for **biochemical oxygen demand**. BOD is a measure of the amount of oxygen needed by bacteria to remove organic material from water.

Table 2. Monthly analysis of filter bed effluent

Month	SS (mg/l)	BOD (mg/l)	Ammonia (mg/l)	Nitrate (mg/l)
April	29.5	18	7.2	8.4
May	27	17	7.6	10.7
June	29.5	19	5.5	10.2
July	21.5	14.5	5.6	13.4
August	25.5	16.5	7.7	14.8
September	25.5	21.5	6.7	9.9
October	31	22	11.4	7.9
November	34.5	28.5	13.5	5.7
December	32.5	35	9.9	4.9
January	35	31	11.2	3.6
February	42	40	12.4	4.0
March	44	35.5	14.4	3.8

Use Table 1 to answer Questions 1–4.

1 Write an account of the ways in which the crude sewage is changed by primary settlement.

2 Write a description of the ways in which the liquid is changed by passing through the filter bed.

3 What percentage of the *original* suspended solids is removed by:
a) primary settlement?
b) bacterial action in the filter bed?

4 What do the figures suggest that the bacteria in the filter bed do to ammonia?

5 Describe how the stones of the filter bed provide a suitable environment for bacterial action.

6 Draw a food web for the filter bed organisms.

MIDGE LARVA (×10)
Eats bacteria and protozoa

FLY LARVA (×10)
Eats bacteria and protozoa

SPRINGTAIL (×10)
Eats bacteria

NEMATODE WORM (×20)
Eats bacteria

SLUDGE WORM (×10)
Eats bacteria

CYCLOPS (×20)
Eats bacteria and protozoa

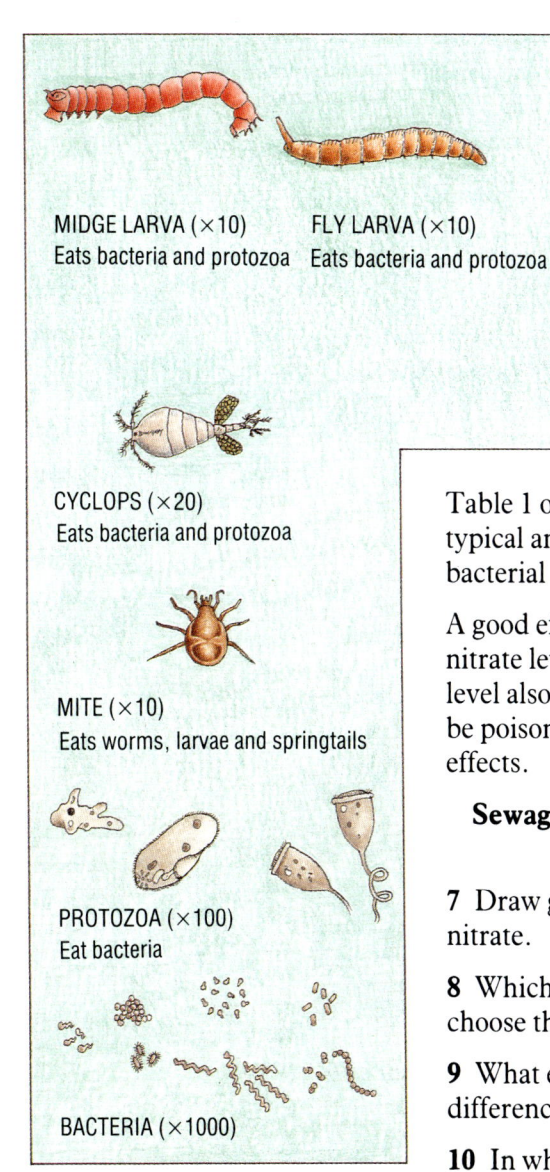

MITE (×10)
Eats worms, larvae and springtails

PROTOZOA (×100)
Eat bacteria

BACTERIA (×1000)

Figure 2. Sewage filter bed organisms.

Table 1 only shows average figures for the whole year. In fact the typical analysis varies because the weather each month affects bacterial action (see Table 2).

A good effluent has low SS, BOD and ammonia levels. As a high nitrate level usually goes with a low ammonia level, a high nitrate level also shows a good effluent. However, high nitrate levels can be poisonous to babies, and can have ecologically damaging effects.

Sewage works should not discharge more than 30 mg/l SS or 20 mg/l BOD.

7 Draw graphs of the monthly figures for SS, BOD, ammonia and nitrate.

8 Which month produces the best effluent? What made you choose this one?

9 What environmental factor do you think will be making most difference to how well the bacteria do their jobs?

10 In which months is this sewage works discharging an effluent that is worse than the required standard?

7.4 Gas from bugs

At a sewage works the filter bed system produces water fit to return to the river. Much of the solid material has settled out as 'sludge'. The sludge digester provides warm, anaerobic conditions needed by the bacteria involved in decomposing the solids.

The sludge contains complex organic chemicals. The first stage in their breakdown produces simple organic acids. If the digester is warm enough, some of these molecules are broken down further to gases, mainly methane and carbon dioxide. If not, the reactions slow down, and the acids build up. If conditions become too acid, no sludge is digested at all. This problem can be corrected by reducing sludge input and by adding lime to neutralize the acid.

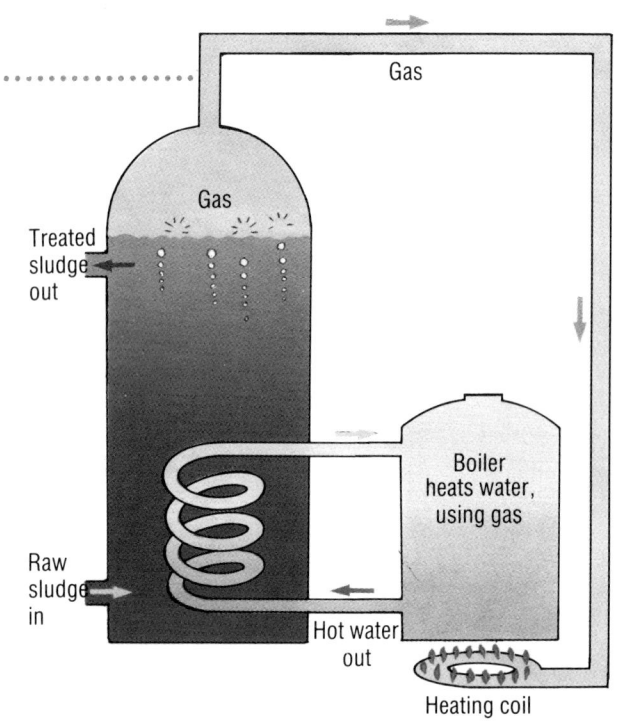

Diagram of digester.

Information about the sludge digester for four months

Month	Gas produced (m^3)	Temperature (°C)	pH
September	29 000	38.3	6.9
October	19 000	36.1	6.5
November	9 000	32.8	6.3
December	30 500	37.8	7.0

When the digester is running well, a lot of methane gas is made. This is burnt to heat the digester to 37 °C. Usually there is enough spare gas to heat the offices and other buildings too. Occasionally the volume of gas produced is so small that the sewage works must buy gas from the Gas Board.

1 Describe the reactions in the sludge digester by naming:
a) the type of organism involved.
b) the substrate it feeds on.
c) the type of respiration occurring.

2 Make a diagram to show the chemical changes in the digester starting with the 'complex molecules'.

3 Which of the products of bacterial action can be used as fuel?

4 What would you expect to be put into the generator shown in Figure 1 for it to produce methane?

5 Use the text above to describe how the change from September to October in the table made it likely that the November figures would occur.

A farm methane generator. In 1988 an enterprising business was set up selling 'farm gas' installations. The animals on the farm contribute to keeping their barns warm, and can even help warm the farm-house.

7.5 Microbes for profit

When you are making substances using microbes, you must consider costs as well as biology. Any business wants to make its products as economically as possible. One of the factors which can be important is the type of process used, that is, the way in which the microbe is made to work.

Bread making

Batch processing is a method in which the microbe and its product are stirred up together. When the microbe has worked long enough the fermentation is stopped. Then the mixture is processed further to separate the product from the rest of the liquid. The microbe can also be recovered and used again, but some may be lost. This method is good if the microbe is part of the end-product, so that there is no need for a separation stage.

In **continuous** processing the microbes are held still, usually in a jelly or on a mesh support. The raw materials are trickled over them and the liquid containing the product is collected at the other end. Purification is much simpler than in batch processing as the product is not mixed up with the microbes. This is particularly useful if the microbes are expensive.

1 Look at the pictures of different processes on this page. Only some use biotechnology.
a) Decide whether each one shows batch or continuous processing.
b) Make a table and record in it the examples of the two types of processing shown in the pictures.

2 Describe the differences between batch and continuous processing.

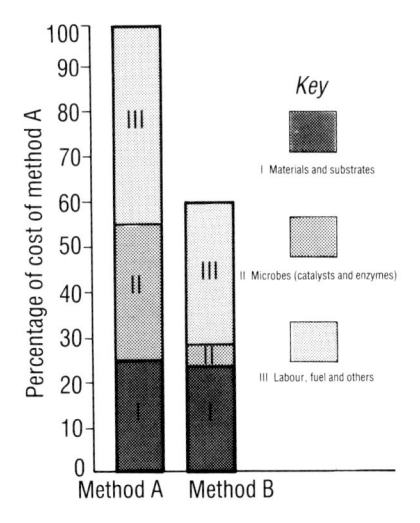

Figure 1. Costs for two ways of making a substance.

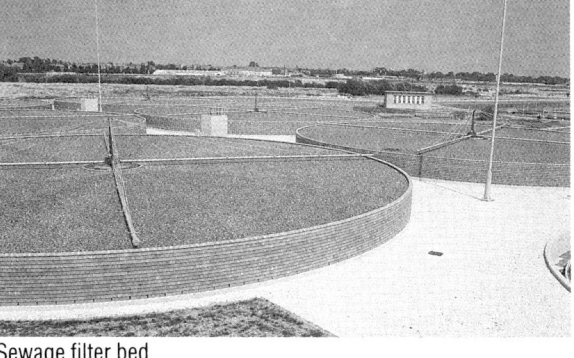

Key
I Materials and substrates
II Microbes (catalysts and enzymes)
III Labour, fuel and others

Sewage filter bed

Figure 1 shows the relative costs of making one substance by batch processing and by continuous processing. The figures show one method to be cheaper than the other. However, some processes do not work equally well with both methods, so economics is only one of the factors to take into account when deciding on a production method.

3 Which of A and B do you think is continuous processing? Give a reason for your answer.

Assembly line

7.6 Sewage and pollution

Millions of gallons of sewage are treated in the U.K. every day. Even so, pollution from sewage can still have important effects on living things. Only careful study of these effects can prevent damage being done. There are two main kinds of sewage:

Industrial effluent (from factories) may contain chemicals, like copper or mercury, that are poisonous, and need special treatment. Some industrial effluent may simply be warm water, e.g. from power stations. Warm water contains less dissolved oxygen than cold water.

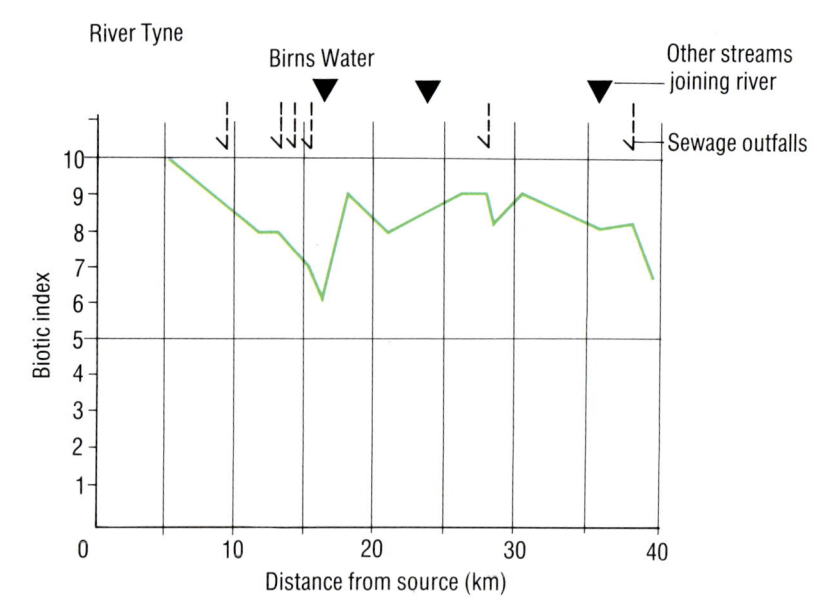

Figure 1. Sewage outfalls and biotic index along the River Tyne.

Figure 2. A simple version of a biotic index.

Numbers of *types* present	Most important types to notice		Biotic index
Many	Mayfly	Stonefly	High 10–8 Very clean
Not quite so many	*Gammarus*	Caddis fly	7–5 Note: *no* mayflies or stoneflies
Few	*Asellus* (waterlouse)		4–3 Note: *no* caddis or *Gammarus*
Very few	Chironomid	*Tubifex* worms	Low 2–1 Polluted, *no Asellus*
None			0 Badly polluted

Domestic sewage (from houses, schools, shops etc.) is less likely to be poisonous, but may reduce the amount of oxygen dissolved in the water.

Even the 'clean' water from a sewage works can influence wildlife in the river or sea near the **outfall**. This is the place where the sewage works discharges treated water.

One way of measuring the effect of sewage on a community of organisms living in water is to look closely at the variety of types present. We can compare communities upstream and downstream of the sewage outfall in a river.

To compare communities, water board biologists use a short guide called a **biotic index**. This is a checklist of water creatures known to live in freshwater in certain conditions. These creatures are called **indicator organisms**.

Figure 2 shows how a simple biotic index works.

1 What does a high biotic index tell you about a community, and what does this suggest about the water?

2 Look at Figure 1. What effect does sewage outfall have on the biotic index in the River Tyne?

3 How is the biotic index of the River Tyne affected by the Birns Water joining the river?

4 Suggest an explanation for this effect.

5 Look at Figure 3. What happens to the biotic index of the River Allan at the two outfalls? Is this what you would expect?

Another way of studying the effect of sewage is to study one particular group of bacteria, and count the numbers of them in the water.

'Faecal coliform' bacteria normally live in the human intestine, and cannot survive for long in a freshwater environment. If they are found in a pond or river, it must be polluted with domestic sewage. High levels of sewage pollution may put public health at risk, since disease bacteria may be present along with the normal sewage bacteria.

As well as looking revolting, sewage damages the community of organisms that live in the river. The large numbers of bacteria in the water use up the oxygen and some animals cannot survive.

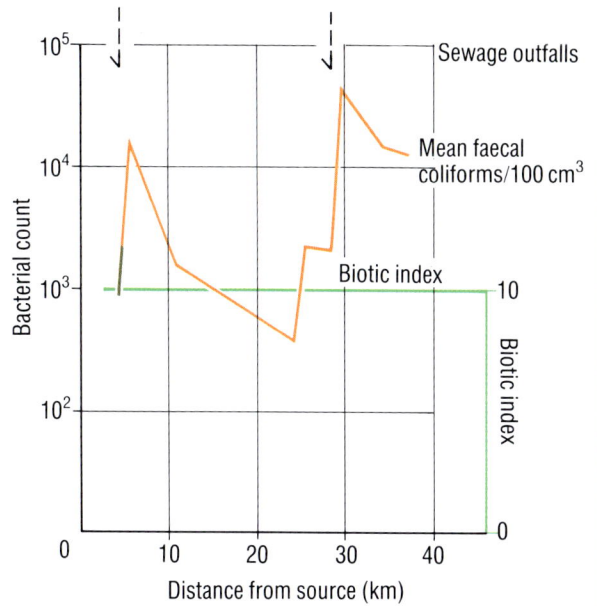

Figure 3. Biotic index and bacterial counts along the River Allan.

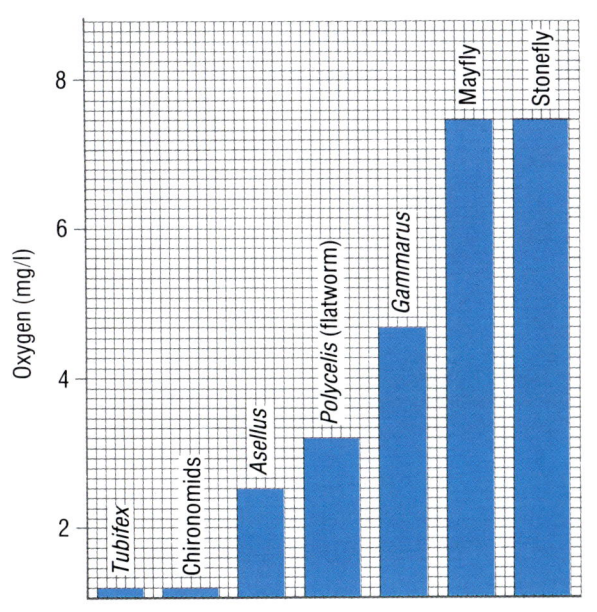

Figure 4. Oxygen requirements of some invertebrates.

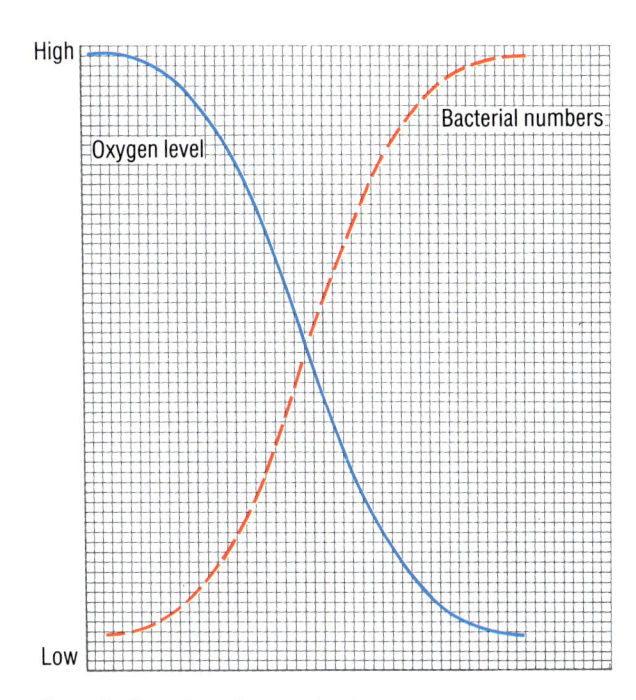

Figure 5. Bacteria and oxygen level.

6 Look at Figure 3. Describe the changes in the mean faecal coliform count, and suggest causes of increased levels.

7 Describe what Figure 4 shows about the oxygen needs of stoneflies and mayflies compared with *Tubifex*.

8 Use Figure 5 and your answer to Question 7 to explain why bacteria from sewage can make the biotic index of a river community drop.

7.7 The insulin story

Although Benny is quite young, he has learned to inject himself every day with a dose of insulin. Benny is a **diabetic**. This means his body cannot make **insulin**, a chemical produced in the pancreas which normally controls the level of sugar in the blood. Without it, he could go into a coma and die. About one child in every thousand suffers from diabetes.

Insulin was first used to save human life in 1922. A small boy who was critically ill with diabetes was given an injection of an extract from an animal's pancreas. Nowadays, new improved forms of insulin are manufactured on an industrial scale.

Until recently, most of the insulin for diabetics came from the pancreas of animals slaughtered for meat. This meant that the supply of insulin was controlled by the demand for meat rather than the needs of diabetics. Another problem was that some people are allergic to animal insulin. The ideal solution is human insulin, which can now be produced by the technique of **genetic engineering**.

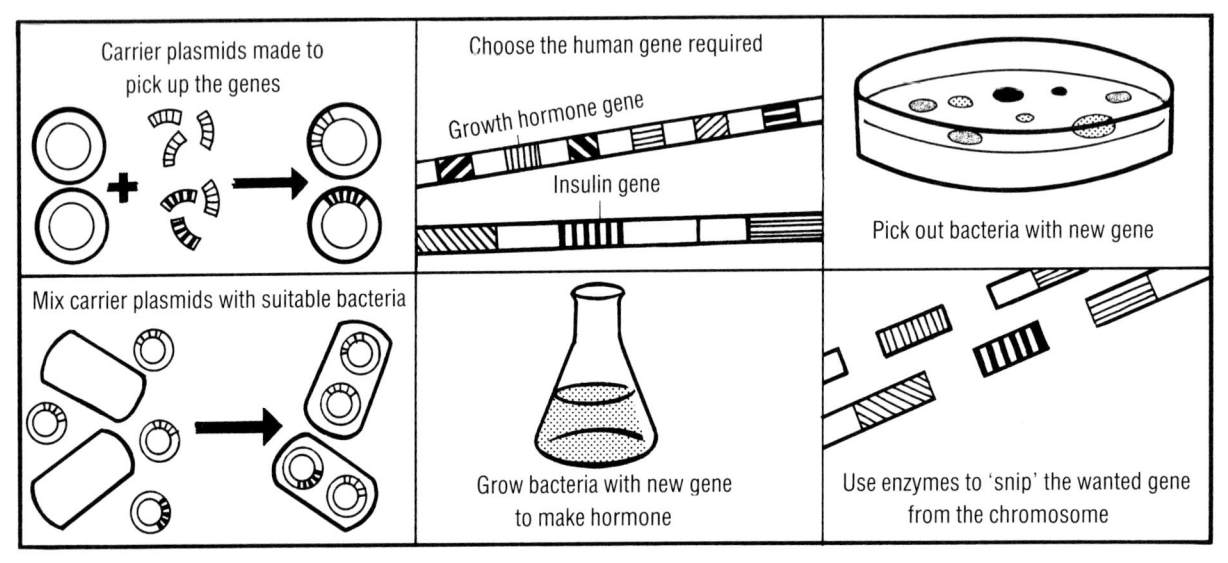

Some stages in changing a bacterium so that it will make human insulin. They are **not** in the right order.

- Carrier plasmids made to pick up the genes
- Choose the human gene required (Growth hormone gene, Insulin gene)
- Pick out bacteria with new gene
- Mix carrier plasmids with suitable bacteria
- Grow bacteria with new gene to make hormone
- Use enzymes to 'snip' the wanted gene from the chromosome

In this case, bacterial cells are modified, so each cell makes human insulin. The insulin is then extracted and purified. Perhaps the most interesting thing about this technique is that a human gene can be introduced into a bacterial cell and still work. The insulin produced is identical to normal human insulin.

Insulin cannot be taken by mouth because it would be broken down by the digestive system. Until now it has had to be injected. However, diabetics may soon be using a nasal spray which contains insulin. When insulin is sprayed into the nostrils, it is absorbed into the blood stream through the fine membranes of the nose.

Benny's diabetes may never actually be cured, but with the production of pure human insulin by genetic engineering techniques, and the nasal spray taking the place of the syringe, life for Benny will at least become safer and easier.

1 How was insulin first used on humans?

2 Until recently, where did most of the insulin required by diabetics come from? Give two disadvantages of this source.

3 Study the diagrams above. Work out what the correct order must be. Use the diagrams to help you write a brief account of the stages in making human insulin by genetic engineering.

4 What is the main advantage of the insulin that is produced by genetic engineering?

7.8 Should it be allowed?

Despite the advantages of the new genetic engineering techniques many people are afraid that scientists will try out experiments without taking enough safety precautions.

SCIENTISTS KNOW BEST!

Some of the dangers

The bacteria used are usually made resistant to antibiotics. This helps scientists to pick out the ones that have the new genes in them. This resistance might be passed on to other bacteria which cause serious diseases. These diseases would then become very hard to cure.

Any 'fast-growth' genes put into crops might escape into wild plants and upset the ecosystem in unpredictable ways.

NO ONE SHOULD MEDDLE WITH LIVING THINGS!

WITHOUT NEW CROPS PEOPLE DIE!!

While working with bacteria, scientists might make dangerous new disease-causing or cancer-causing forms. These could escape from the laboratory to damage plants or animals.

A human gene is usually transferred to a microbe for study. This lets it act without its normal controls. If the microbe infects a human being the gene, now uncontrolled, may be dangerous.

Project 1
Some plant roots carry nodules which contain bacteria. These allow the plants to fix nitrogen from the air, instead of needing nitrate from the soil. If the genes which control nitrogen fixation could be engineered into crop plants, more food could be grown with smaller amounts of fertilizer and less pollution.

Project 2
Scientists want to map out the whole set of genes carried on human chromosomes. This would help in the diagnosis of inherited diseases. One of the stages would involve copying relatively large fragments of human chromosomes into microbes.

Watchdog committees have been set up to monitor gene transfer experiments, especially where the experimental organisms grow outdoors rather than in laboratories.

You are on a watchdog committee.

1 Do you want Project 1 to go ahead? Give reasons for your answer.

2 Do you want Project 2 to go ahead? Explain why.

3 What groups of people do you think ought to be represented on a watchdog committee?

4 Do you think that a watchdog committee is likely to be able to control the experiments that scientists do? Give reasons for your answers.

Numerical Answers

UNIT 1

1.1
1 a 500
   b 2500
2 a 50 g
   b 60
3 a 0.10 g
   b 20 000 bees
4 a 100
   b 400
5 a 20 000 m^3
   b 200
   c 6
   d 1200
6 a 50 m^3
   b 50 000
   c 75
   d 7.5
   e 375 000

1.3
1 5
2 5/20 = 25%
3 90%

1.5 Completed Table 2.

Seaweed species	Where found (vertical height above low water, metres)	
	Highest point	Lowest point
Serrated wrack	0.50	0
Kelp	0.15	0
Knotted wrack	1.55	0.45
Spiral wrack	2.60	1.45
Channeled wrack	3.00	2.25
Bladder wrack	1.90	0.40

1.6 4 120 cm
1

1.8

1939	1940	1941	1942	1943
100	300	600	1300	1500

1.9
1 a 3920 MJ
  b 392 MJ
  c 10%
  d 90%
4 a 276 900 MJ
  b 439 MJ   (1.9 Continued on p.105)

1.4

Level	Name	Numbers		Weights = biomass		
		in group	Total at level	One organism × number	of group	Total at level
Plants (= producers)	Saw wrack	27	148	19 × 27	513	1446.6
	Egg wrack	4		120 × 4	480	
	Red weed	83		4.4 × 83	365.2	
	Corallina	34		2.6 × 34	88.4	
Herbivores and detritus feeders (= first consumers)	Winkles	87	174	1.3 × 87	113.1	206.1
	Top shell	45		1.6 × 45	72	
	Sandhopper	42		0.5 × 42	21	
Carnivores (= second consumers)	Whelks	15	28	3.6 × 15	54	104.4
	Starfish	2		—	2.8	
	Scale worm	5		2.0 × 5	10	
	Hermit crab	6		—	37.6	

Note: If whelk shells are not counted weight is 1.1 × 15 = 16.5 g and total at level is 66.9 g.

1.9 (cont.)	5	a	In, tertiary 200 MJ
		b	Percentage passed on, primary 9.8% secondary 9.1% tertiary 1%
		c	Percentage used, secondary 90.9%
	6	a	25%
		b	0.8%
1.13	1	a	104.3
		b	102
	2	a	23.5%
		b	20.0%

UNIT 2

2.2 2

	Percentage oil	Percentage waste
Soya	18.4	1.6
Cotton seed	20	38.4
Groundnuts	45.8	4.2
Sunflower	38	2.0
Rape seed	39.1	1.8

2.4 6 Any of: A + B, C + D, E + F, G + H, I + J, K + L, M + N, O + P.

7 Any pair from above not used before.

8 Any of: A + C, B + D, E + G, F + H, I + K, J + L, M + O, N + P.

9 A, E

2.7 1 0
5 40 units
6 0.5%, 60 units. 1.0%, 80 units
10 1000 p.p.m. CO_2
11 25 °C
12 5.5 kg/m²

UNIT 3

3.4 6 Use average of results of C and D.

	Meat	Cucumber	Egg	Rice
a	6.7 g	9.6 g	7.5 g	1.2 g
b	67%	96%	75%	12%

3.6 1

	3	4	5
	3500	**3400**	3000
	800	1000	200
	300	500	300
	4600	**4900**	3500
	2500	1200	600
	1500	3000	1000
	500	600	400
	100	100	**1500**
	4600	4900	**3500**

3 Seven times
4 4000 cm³
5 3 days
6 2 days

UNIT 4

4.6 2 48 s or 0.8 min
3 37 °C

4.8 1 60 °C, pH 6

4

	A	D
Warm (40 °C)	59%	44%
Medium (50 °C)	41%	62%
Hot (60 °C)	17%	75%

UNIT 5

5.1 2 c 313 kJ food (100%)
281.3 kJ heat and movement (89.8%)
31.7 kJ wastes (10.2%)

4 30.76% (30.8%)

5.2 1 a 1 hour
b 1/5 hour = 12 min

2 4562 kJ

5.3 2 2400 g
3 25%, 600 g
5 690 g
6 69%, 476 g

5.4   **4**

Percentage CO_2	Breaths per minute	Volume of each breath (cm^3)	Total air volume per minute (cm^3)	Extra air volume per minute (cm^3)	Percentage increase
0.04	72	19	1368	–	–
4.2	96	25	2400	1032	75
8.6	97	29	2813	1445	105

5.6   **4**

Name of sport	Diagram of sites and description code	Cause of damage		
		Equipment	Falls	Twists
Football	1 F	?	+	+
Hockey	3 D	+	?	+
Swimming	2 A	–	–	–
Rugby	6 E	?	+	+
Badminton	5 B	+	?	+
Judo	4 C	–	+	+

? means that knowledge of the game suggests these are possible but they are not in the text.

5.8   **5 a** 80 cm^3 (Pat's), 60 cm^3 (Chris's)
        b Pat 125 beats per minute, Chris 166.6 (167) beats per minute.

5.9   **1** 60, 80, 100 and 120 W
      2 140, 160 and 200 W
      8 164 W

6.3   **3** 50%

6.4   **5 a** 1 in 4 (1/4)
        b 1 in 2 (1/2)
        c 1 in 4 (1/4)

6.7   **4 a** 87%
        b 13%
      7 0
      8 a 250 mSv

7.2   **1** 16, 32, 64, 128, 256
      3 65 536

7.3   **3 a** 60%
        b 30%

Index

acid rain 20, 21
acidity 20, 21, 30, 31, 40, 98
activity 63, 69, 70, 71
adaptation 38
agar 27
air 29, 30, 34, 35, 52, 66, 67, 77
alginate 27
alkalinity 30, 31, 40, 61
aluminium 21
amino acids 37, 40, 41
amniocentesis 85–87
amylase 40, 41, 60
anaemia 84
antibiotic 92, 103
apples 32, 33
Ascophyllum 27
atoms 36, 37

bacteria 48, 60, 92, 96, 97, 102, 103
batch processing 99
bicarbonate indicator 30, 31
bile 40, 41
biochemical oxygen demand 96, 97
biomass 9
biotechnology 92, 93, 99
biotic index 100, 101
birth weight 79
blood 44, 45, 50, 51, 68, 79, 84, 85, 102
boron 27
breathing 66, 67, 76, 77
breeding programme 88, 89

cadmium 79
cancer 90, 103
carbon dioxide 4, 20, 30, 34, 35, 37, 50, 66, 67, 98
carnivores 9, 13, 16
cells 50, 51, 53–55, 94, 95
cell membrane 51
chemical energy 54, 56
chromosome 82–87, 90, 103
clay 28, 29
cobalt 27
cold blooded animals 56, 58

colon 41
communities 8, 9, 16, 17, 100, 101
competition 18, 19
compounds 36
consumers 9, 17
continuous processing 99
copper 21, 27, 100
crops 19, 78, 88, 89, 103
cuttings 32, 33
CVS (chorionic villus sampling) 86, 87

Daphnia 18
detritus feeders 9
diabetes 102
dialysis 44, 45
diarrhoea 46, 47
diet 64, 65, 68
dieting 64, 65
diffusion 50
digestion 37, 40, 41
dilution plating 94, 95
direct counting 94, 95
disease 101, 103
disease resistance 88, 89
diseases, inherited 82–87
distribution 6–11, 48, 49
DNA 90, 91
Down's syndrome 87
Drosophila 91
Duchenne muscular dystrophy 82, 83
duodenum 40, 41

ecosystems 20, 100
effluent 97, 100, 101
eggs (egg-cells) 38, 39, 82, 88–90
electricity 54
elements 36
embryo 85, 86
energy 16, 17, 36, 54–57, 62–65
environment 49, 52, 53, 78, 101
enzymes 40, 41, 59–61
estimate 2, 42

faeces 46, 62
fat 37, 40, 41, 64
fatty acids 40, 41
fermentation 92, 99
fertilization 38, 39, 82, 83
fertilizer 27
fish 12, 13, 21, 38, 39
fitness 68–75
foetus 86, 87
food 16–19, 36, 37, 40–42, 56, 62–65
food web 14, 16, 17
fruit flies 91
fungi 60, 92

gametes 38
gas exchange 50
genes 82–88, 94, 103
genetic engineering 94, 95, 102, 103
genetics 78, 82–89
germination 28, 29
glucose 41
glycerol 40, 41
glycogen 65
grafting 33
grass 6, 7, 27
gut 40, 41

heart 68, 69, 74–77
heart disease 68, 69, 74, 75
heat 54, 56, 57, 62
herbivores 9, 13, 16
humidity 48, 49

ileum 40
indicator organisms 100, 101
inheritance 80–87
injury 70, 71, 73
insects 14, 58
insulin 102
iodine 27
iron 27

kidney 44, 45
kidney machine 44, 45

lactate 77
large intestine 41
lead 79
light 4, 5, 16, 19, 28–31, 34, 35, 48, 49, 54
lipase 40
lungs 77

maltose 37, 40, 60
mercury 100
metabolic cage 62
metals 27, 79
methane 98
microbes 92–95, 98, 99, 103
minerals 4, 5, 19, 21, 27
miscarriage 86, 87
molecules 36, 37
movement 58, 62, 68–77, 83
muscle 58, 65, 72, 73
mutagen 91
mutation 90, 91

nitrate 96, 97, 103
nitrogen 66, 103

oesophagus 40
oil 22, 23, 26
omnivores 13
osmosis 51
osmotic potential 53
oxygen 12, 34, 35, 50, 52, 65–67, 96, 100

pectolase 60
peristalsis 40
pH 20, 40, 41, 60, 61
pheasants 15
photosynthesis 30, 31, 34, 35, 55
phytoplankton 4, 5

placenta 86, 87
plankton 4, 5
plant growth 28, 29, 34, 35
plant products 25, 26, 27
plantain 6, 7
pollination 32, 33, 88
pollution 20–23, 93, 100, 101
population 15
potassium 45
predators 15
pregnancy 85–87
producers 9, 17
protease 60, 61
protein 37, 40, 41, 60, 65
pulse rate 74–77
pyramid of biomass 9
pyramid of numbers 13

quadrat 6, 7

radiation 90, 91
rape seed 26
reproduction 32, 33, 38, 39
respiration 31, 37, 54, 56
rotifer 18

salinity 52, 53
salt 52, 53
salt marsh 52, 53
sampling 2, 3, 6, 7
sand 28, 29
seashore 8–11, 52, 53
seaweeds 10, 11, 27
seedlings 28, 29
seeds 19, 28, 29, 32, 33, 78
sewage 22, 23, 96–101
sex-linkage 83
sludge digester 98
small intestine 41
soil 28, 29
soya 26
sperm 38, 39, 83, 90
spider diagrams 27, 93

sport 70, 71
starch 37, 40, 60
stomach 40, 41
strength 72, 73
submarine 67
sucrose 37
sugar 37, 51, 102
sulphur dioxide 20
sunflower 19, 26
suspended solids 96, 97
sweating 46, 47

temperature 5, 12, 28, 29, 35, 48, 49, 56–58, 60, 61
thalassaemia 84, 85
tides 8–11
training 73–75, 77
trampling 6, 7
trypsin 40

ultra-violet light 91
urea 44, 45
urine 46, 47, 62

variation 33, 88, 89

warm blooded animals 56
washing powder 59, 60, 61
water 19, 22, 23, 29, 36, 42–47, 50–53, 64, 65
water balance 44–47, 51–53
water flea 18
weight loss 74–77
X-rays 91

yeast 92

zinc 27, 79
zonation 53
zooplankton 4